The Intersectionality of
Women's Lives and Resistance

Communicating Gender

Series Editors: Diana Bartelli Carlin, Saint Louis University
Nichola D. Gutgold, Pennsylvania State University
Theodore F. Sheckels, Randolph-Macon College

Communicating Gender features original research examining the role gender plays in communication. It encompasses a wide variety of approaches and methodologies to explore theoretically relevant topics pertaining to the interrelation of gender and communication both in the United States and worldwide. This series examines gender issues broadly, ranging from masculine hegemony and gender issues in political culture to media portrayals of women and men and the work/life balance.

Recent titles in the series:

The Intersectionality of Women's Lives and Resistance, edited by Dawn L. Hutchinson and Lori J. Underwood

Misogyny and Media in the Age of Trump, edited by Maria B. Marron

The Rhetorical Arts of Women in Aviation, 1911–1970: Name It and Take It, by Sara Hillin

Food Blogs, Postfeminism, and the Construction of Expertise: Digital Domestics, by Alane Presswood

Developing Women Leaders in the Academy through Enhanced Communication Strategies, edited by Jayne Cubbage

Empowering Women: Global Voices of Rhetorical Influence, by Julia Spiker

Technofeminist Storiographies: Women, Information Technology, and Cultural Representation, by Kristine Blair

Women of the 2016 Election: Voices, Views, and Values, edited by Jennifer Schenk Sacco

Adolescence, Girlhood, and Media Migration: US Teens' Use of Social Media to Negotiate Offline Struggles, by Aimee Rickman

Consuming Agency and Desire in Romance: Stories of Love, Laughter, and Empowerment, by Jenni M. Simon

The Intersectionality of Women's Lives and Resistance

Edited by Dawn L. Hutchinson and
Lori J. Underwood

LEXINGTON BOOKS
Lanham • Boulder • New York • London

Published by Lexington Books
An imprint of The Rowman & Littlefield Publishing Group, Inc.
4501 Forbes Boulevard, Suite 200, Lanham, Maryland 20706
www.rowman.com

6 Tinworth Street, London SE11 5AL

British Library Cataloguing in Publication Information Available

Library of Congress Cataloging-in-Publication Data

Names: Hutchinson, Dawn L., editor. | Underwood, Lori J., editor.
Title: The intersectionality of women's lives and resistance / edited by Dawn L. Hutchinson and Lori J. Underwood.
Description: Lanham : Lexington Books, [2020] | Series: Communicating gender | Includes bibliographical references and index.
Identifiers: LCCN 2019055124 (print) | LCCN 2019055125 (ebook) | ISBN 9781793613707 (cloth) | ISBN 9781793613721 (paper) | ISBN 9781793613714 (epub)
Subjects: LCSH: Women--Social conditions. | Intersectionality (Sociology)
Classification: LCC HQ1150 .I59 2020 (print) | LCC HQ1150 (ebook) | DDC 305.4--dc23
LC record available at https://lccn.loc.gov/2019055124

Contents

Introduction

Christopher Newport University College of Arts and Humanities held its 4th annual conference on the Global Status of Women and Girls with Norfolk State University at CNU, March 21–13, 2019. The theme for this year's conference was *Intersectionality: Understanding Women's Lives and Resistance.*

This interdisciplinary conference sought to use the tools of the arts, humanities, social sciences, and other fields to address challenges faced by women and girls around the world, both historically and today. Our 2019 theme marks the 30th anniversary of Kimberlé Crenshaw's use of the term "intersectionality," as well as the 400th anniversary of the first Africans arriving in Hampton and the Jamestown colony in 1619. Given the close proximity of Hampton and Jamestown, this year's conference especially highlighted ways in which gender intersects race, ethnicity, class, sexuality, and other identity markers in complex ways. To this end, we welcomed proposals that used an intersectional approach to understand these subjects as well as the interconnectedness of systems of oppression, power and privilege.

Ten representative papers from the conference have been chosen to be included in these conference proceedings. They were selected to represent the diversity of views presented at the conference. The editors of this volume, Dr. Lori J. Underwood and Dr. Dawn L. Hutchinson, have also edited the first, second, and third annual conference proceedings.

CHAPTERS

The introduction will explain the purpose and theme of the conference and the scope of the papers. The following include the papers that we have accepted.

Chapter 1: Lori J. Underwood, PhD, and Dawn L. Hutchinson, PhD, Christopher Newport University, "Race, Gender, Power, Alterity, and the Black Power Movement." This chapter argues that many of the Black power movements did not confront destructive gender alterity within their own organizations. An unexpected exception to this was the Black Panther Party that emerged in the 1970s.

Chapter 2: Gaius Jatau, PhD, Kaduna State University, "Poverty and the Challenges of Women's Participation in Nigerian Politics." The chapter argues that the limited participation of Nigerian women in the political progress has brought stagnation in the political development of women and perhaps the Nigerian nation. It further posits that in spite of the contributions of women to the development of their societies, they are being deliberately excluded from contemporary Nigerian politics. This chapter posits some possible solutions.

Chapter 3: Jason Ray Carney, PhD, Christopher Newport University, "Her Evolution from Terrorized Victim to Psycho-kinetic Madwoman: A Survey of Gothic Heroines." This chapter is about the Gothic heroine. The Gothic is a category of feminist activist literature, art, and film that delivers its aesthetic effect through a two-part process of dramatically staged uncreation or "de-reification." In this process, the "ordinary" or dominant patriarchal order is troubled and exposed as historically contingent: first, the Gothic work establishes an effect of reality and then, second, it stages convincing violations of this effect of reality.

Chapter 4: Ursula Scheidegger, PhD, University of the Witwatersrand, "Democracy and the Limitations on Women's Rights." This chapter discusses the shortcomings of democracy with respect to women's rights and representation. It uses the struggle of Swiss women for the right to vote and participate in politics as its case study. The chapter examines two core features of democracy, representation and the vote, and argues that a set of overarching not negotiable rights and values such as human rights and personal freedoms are critical safeguards in order to protect democracies from powerful interests.

Chapter 5: Geovani Ramirez, PhD Candidate, UNC Chapel Hill, "Ruiz de Burton's Inviolable Californios and Roguish Anglos in *The Squatter and the Don* and *Who Would Have Thought It?*" As an Old World colonialist and proponent of a New World colonialism inclusive of Californios, Ruiz de Burton is at odds with historically marginalized minorities, and her colonialist status and attitudes distinguish her novels from narratives of resistance most commonly thought to inform Mexican-heritage people's experiences in the US. In this chapter, Ramirez argues that Ruiz de Burton disidentifies with Anglo-Americans to promote a narrative of a white, culturally refined, and morally superior Mexican-heritage aristocratic class fit to rule in the US Southwest. Furthermore, she explores how Ruiz de Burton reinforces patriarchal notions about women's vulnerabilities and natural place within the domestic sphere in order to promote Californios' rights.

Chapter 6: Patricia Hopkins, PhD, Christopher Newport University, "Violence and the Black Female Body: Deconstructing Images of Rape in Toni Morrison's *Beloved.*" In this chapter, Hopkins contends that Toni Morrison's post-modern novel, *Beloved*, is apropos for both exploring violence and the black female body in literature, as well as redefining rape in terms that include images of the violated black female body.

Chapter 7: James Cornette, MA, Christopher Newport University, "Resist, Survive, Endure: Empowered Female Characters in Patrick O'Brian's Aubrey/Maturin Novels." This chapter is about Patrick O'Brian's Aubrey/Maturin novels. O'Brian's fiction provides a window into the status and treatment of women and girls in the early nineteenth century, as he explores the era's emerging awareness of the rights of women as a vital element in the struggle against tyranny.

Chapter 8: Sandra Williamson-Ashe, PhD, Norfolk State University, "A Distinct Set of Characteristics for Black Women at an HBCU: Tortured by Slavery-Shaped by Intersectionality-Liberated into Othermothering." This chapter argues that specific characteristics built from enslavement and shaped by intersectionality uniquely coalesce to image Black women at historically black colleges and universities (HBCU) as "othermothering." Black women provide university services for students delineated as going above and beyond the call of duty. Survival of slavery created the Black woman's strengths, appreciated today as principals, navigators, artist, and architects.

Chapter 9: Mujtaba Ali Muhammad, PhD candidate, and Sa'ad Deen Sa'ad, Walden University, "Forced Migration: Boko Haram's Induced Migration and the Plight of Women and Young Girls in Northern Nigeria." This chapter explores the genesis of the forced migration of the victims of "Jama'atu Ahlussunnah Lidda'awati wal jihad," Boko Haram's terrorist group conflict in Northern Nigeria. The author highlights how the insurgency forced the victims into migration and the role played by the Nigerian army in forcing these internally displaced persons (IDPs) into migration.

Chapter One

Race, Gender, Power, Alterity, and the Black Power Movement

Lori J. Underwood and Dawn L. Hutchinson

Women who worked toward social change during the civil rights movement in America had multiple goals. Organizers like Ella Baker did not distinguish between feminist goals and the goals they had for the civil rights movement. Black feminists have long recognized that different forms of discrimination existed in their lives, including racism, classism, and sexism, and that they needed to form a discourse about these overlapping realities. Darlene Clark Hine's "culture of dissemblance," Deborah K. King's "multiple jeopardy," Patricia Hill Collins' "insider-outsider," Evelyn Brooks Higginbotham's "metalanguage of race," and Kimberlé Crenshaw's "intersectionality" were employed to make sense of these inter-related spheres of existence.[1] Activist women began working on legislation to eliminate segregation and discrimination in many areas of society well before the civil rights era began. Yet, there appeared to be a disconnect for the women working specifically in the Black power movement.

Women working in the Black power movement, while engaged in progress toward black empowerment, were also engaged in a struggle for equality within their own movement. For instance, Ruby Doris Smith Robinson, the Executive Secretary of the Student Nonviolent Coordinating Committee (SNCC), initially accepted the leadership of men in the movement, but later began to question leaders when they claimed that women were doing the "men's job."[2] Religious movements in the Black power movement, like the Nation of Islam (NOI), reinforced patriarchal attitudes that contributed to the continuation of the oppression of women. Elijah Muhammad's focus was on the self-sufficiency of the community; as part of this mission, he taught that a stable family was central to societal success. His vision of family tended to be a patriarchal one. An examination of the rhetoric of Malcolm X shows that his gender ideology shifted over time, thanks to many of the women that he collaborated with in radical movements.[3]

ALTERITY

While the Black power movement was designed to fight alterity, because of a number of religious and cultural factors, some leaders unconsciously enforced alterity of a different kind. Stokely Carmichael's SNCC, the Nation of Islam, and the Nation of Yahweh reinforced alterity, while the Black Panther for Self-Defense (BPP) developed ways to fight it. Alterity, or "othering" can come in two distinct forms; constructive and destructive. The term constructive alterity can be somewhat misleading. Constructive does not imply that alterity in this sense is necessarily a positive force or contributes to good relations between groups. Indeed, constructive alterity is still divisive in that it promotes divisiveness over unity. By constructive alterity, we mean limited to constructing one's own sense of identity. One of the authors of this paper is a mixed race, Catholic, heterosexual, vegetarian working mother who is a Kantian philosopher and a dean. These all make up her identity, her othering herself from those without those traits. This othering is how she defines who she is.

A similar use of constructive alterity is employed by Malcolm X in his "Black Man's History" speech in December 1962:

> We don't separate our color from our religion. The white man doesn't. The white man never has separated Christianity from white, nor has he separated the white man from Christianity. When you hear the white man bragging, "I'm a Christian," he's bragging about being a white man. Then you have the Negro. When he is bragging about being a Christian, he's bragging that he's a white man, or he wants to be white, and usually those Negroes who brag like that, I think you have to agree, in their songs and the things they sing in church, they show that they have a greater desire to be white than anything else. . . . So many people, especially our people, get resentful when they hear me say something like this. But rather than get resentful all they have to do is think back on many of the songs and much of the teachings and the doctrines that they were taught while they were going to church and they'll have to agree that it was all designed to make us look down on black and up at white.[4]

It should be noted that this speech was given while Malcolm X was still a member of the Nation of Islam. He converted to Islam before his death and his religious view were greatly altered as a result. Nevertheless, one of the primary goals of the "Black Man's History" speech was to establish a foundation for constructive alterity. It was intended to express how black people are distinct from white Christians: he points out differences in skin color, songs, rituals, and power structures. The message is one of pride and identity construction. There is nothing in this particular speech guided toward the incitement of violence. Granted, Malcolm X does predict God will judge white people for the evil they have wrought, but his recommendation for his race is separation, not revenge. The message remains grounded in constructive, rather than devolving into destructive alterity.

While constructive alterity is not always a positive force in society in that it promotes focus on what divides rather than what unites us, constructive alterity alone does not serve as a motivation for acts of violence or oppression. Constructive alterity may well be an inevitable part of the human experience. To feel secure in whom we are, it may be psychologically necessary to establishing within that identity a strong definition of who we are not. It is only when the process of defining oneself and recognizing what is other leads to fear and hatred of the other that the motivation for violence or social/political alienation of the "othered" group tends to arise. This is the movement from constructive to destructive alterity.

Destructive alterity not only draws a distinction between the subject's identity group and the group that is "other," it also establishes a fear or perception of superiority within the members of the subject group that their identity, existence, or dominance is endangered by the difference or the empowerment of the alteritous group. That fear can develop into hatred that escalates into a motivation to violence or legal or social marginalization. There is not always a direct connection between the person or persons who develop the alteritous ideology and the individuals who carry out the actions motivated by it. It is difficult to define a precise moment when alterity moves from constructive to destructive, but when preservation of self is seen as requiring harm or marginalization of the other, it is certain that the transition has occurred.

Consider the infamous inaugural address given by Alabama governor George Wallace on January 14, 1963. It is now infamously known as the "Segregation now, segregation forever" speech because of its vehement rejection of federal efforts to enforce the integration of public schools mandated by the landmark U.S. Supreme Court case *Brown v. Board of Education of Topeka*. Wallace not only drew a strict distinction between his white constituents and those who would take their freedom, he called upon the people of Alabama to fight to prevent integration.

> And so it was meant in our racial lives . . . each race, within its own framework has the freedom to teach . . . to instruct . . . to develop . . . to ask for and receive deserved help from others of separate racial stations. This is the great freedom of our American founding fathers . . . but if we amalgamate into the one unit as advocated by the communist philosophers . . . then the enrichment of our lives . . . the freedom for our development . . . is gone forever. We become,

therefore, a mongrel unit of one under a single all powerful government . . .
and we stand for everything . . . and for nothing.[5]

One of the central meeting points for the anti-segregationist civil rights organizers in Birmingham was the Sixteenth Street Baptist Church. On Sunday, September 15, 1963, at 10:22 a.m. a bomb shook the building killing four African American girls; one 11-year-old and three 14-year-olds. The bombing was later attributed to men affiliated with the Ku Klux Klan. Witnesses later testified that one of the men bragged about the murders and wore them "like a badge of honor." Because of problems with access to evidence and witnesses, no one was successfully tried for the crime until 1977.[6]

The bombing of the church was an act of domestic terrorism. The building target was symbolic; it was a known central meeting place for civil rights groups. The bombing time, a Sunday morning between Sunday school and morning services, was chosen because there was a strong likelihood that people would be inside the building. There were targets of opportunity that struck fear in the intended victims of the message; in this case those who would protest for integration and other civil rights. The ideology of alterity espoused in Wallace's speech had motivated violent action before in the beating of the Freedom Riders and numerous other incidents of targeted ideologically motivated violence. Wallace's call to fight to preserve segregation may have been causally inert in this instance or it may well have bolstered the feeling of fear and hatred that drove the men involved to bomb that church in Birmingham. In either event, this is an example of an alterity dynamic that was destructive.

INTERSECTIONALITY

Women in the Black power movement employed "intersectionality" to make sense of their inter-related spheres of existence as they actively worked toward eliminating segregation and discrimination in many areas of society. Intersectionality is a term that refers to multiple levels of disadvantage a person may encounter as compounded inequalities. These inequalities created obstacles that conventional models were not designed to recognize.[7] The women we are writing about were particularly aware of their overlapping racial and gender identities. Working for equality in one area of their lives was not always consistent with working for equality in another area of their lives. At times, this created discord.

The key question we wish to consider is: At the nexus of alterity and intersectionality, did some of the groups in the Black power movement unconsciously reinforce the kind of destructive alterity on the women in their group that they were fighting against in the civil rights movement? This destructive alterity may have been in the form of violence, but in many cases, it was in the form of marginalization and/or a perception of inferiority to the men in the group(s).

WOMEN IN CARMICHAEL'S SNCC

The Student Non-Violent Coordinating Committee, founded in the 1960s was an entry point into the public side of the civil rights movement for many black college students. Initially focused on Judeo-Christian principles of nonviolence and justice, the movement progressed into a call for freedom from oppression. Eventually as the movement spread north, many white college students joined the cause and white and black women found their assignments were very different. "Routine sexual harassment undercut the political effectiveness of women staff members. In this context some Black women protested directly against gender bias, a strategy that white women did not imitate."[8] However, many "Black women staff members deferred to the leadership of Black men within SNCC because they regarded the advancement of Black men as a crucial ingredient in their own destiny as Black women. In this regard they resembled the civil rights movement as a whole."[9] In 1964, SNCC leader Stokely Carmichael is said to have declared that "the only position for women in the movement is 'prone.'" Now, being a supporter of women in the movement, his words may have been tongue-in-cheek, but that he said them reveals an audience that was receptive, which exposes an element of destructive alterity within the movement—conscious or not.

Not all women in the movement agreed that women should follow prescribed gender norms. One notable example was Ella Baker. She was a role model for many women in the movement. Her organizational skills were integral to the success of the early movement, and many of her early speeches motivated young activists like Diane Nash to become engaged in the movement.[10] Young women in the BPM also observed that Baker offered them an "alternative view of womanhood" as activists.[11] While she dressed conservatively and demonstrated proper southern manners, Baker spoke her mind firmly. She was as comfortable in the dining room discussing issues with the men as she was in the kitchen doing the same. In this way, she made more space for other women in the movement.[12] Another example was Bernice Johnson, who risked expulsion from Albany State due to her protest activity. Baker and Johnson were respected by all members of the movement and became role models for other women.[13] Although central to SNCC activism, the women in the movement were not treated as equal to men; they were "othered." Their contributions were recognized by members at the time, but their legacy has had to be recovered.[14]

WOMEN IN NATION OF ISLAM

Elijah Muhammad's focus was on the self-sufficiency of the Nation of Islam. He intended the Nation to be a separatist religion. His followers went on to create independent businesses and communities so they would not have to rely on former slaveholders. Muhammad's gender ideology was informed by his understanding of the role of the family. Seeing the family as central to the success of an independent community, Muhammad taught that women needed to be wives and mothers.[15] He taught that women required the protection of men in the community.[16] He taught that this control was central to the restoration of men as providers and patriarchs of their families.[17]

The publication of the Moynihan Report in 1966 may have served to strengthen the resolve of this control. Moynihan's report, drawing from the 1939 book *The Negro Family* by sociologist Franklin Frazier, claimed that too many black female heads of households (a matriarchy) was the cause of poverty and family disorganization.[18] Moyniham argued that young black boys needed strong male role models. There was an outcry from many quarters in the black community. Some in the Black Panther Party argued that black women were unwittingly working together with white men to oppress black men.[19] Black feminists had a variety of responses, but all of them reassessed the concept of matriarchy. Objecting to Moynihan's conclusions, Frances Beale of SNCC wrote that black women, like black men, needed to be able to work in public life to "fight the enemy."[20] While Elijah Muhammad had been a proponent of strong male role models for many years, this report gave him additional leverage to continue his policy of tight control of women.

As part of this control, women were expected to adhere to a modest dress code, cover their hair, and take care of their husband and children. They were also required to attend Nation of Islam events and Muslim Girls Training classes regularly. In the classes, women were taught proper homemaking skills and Nation of Islam rules.[21] They were taught that women were the primary educators of the children, and thus the people who shaped how the future generations understood the religion. The education and care of the children was the responsibility of the whole community.[22] Nation women were taught that it was their choices and skills that were the key to their husband's success.[23]

Many of the Nation women did not perceive themselves to be under the control of the men in the movement. Many had home businesses; they worked as seamstresses, fish marketers, cooks, and caterers, which offered them control of their finances.[24] Others pursued an education and worked outside of the home, or even outside of the community in educational or service jobs.[25] Some women worked as teachers, daycare workers, factory employees, and domestic workers during the 1960s.[26] They saw themselves as serving the mission of the Nation of Islam to help the community remain self-sufficient. The women that worked on the editorial staff of *Muhammad Speaks*, the official mouthpiece of the prophet, openly disagreed with the prophet's teachings. There are articles that challenge official Nation policy that were published by his staff of women writers without any disagreement from him.[27] For example, Tynetta Deanar, Muhammad's secretary, wrote that women were the underlying secret of the Nation's success. She said, "Actually, it isn't a secret, for her extraordinary talents are known; and without her, man would be eating out of crude pots, perhaps even with their fingers, sitting on stone benches and sleeping on hard wooden floors."[28] Deanar chose a pro-womanist reading of Muhammad's policies. Yet, in many of these cases, the reader had to read between the lines to find these disagreements.

The rhetoric of Malcolm X shows that his gender ideology shifted from being in-line with Elijah Muhammad to being more inclusive over time. Many of the women that he collaborated with in radical movements are responsible for helping to broaden his views.[29] Malcolm X joined the Nation of Islam in 1952, after many discussions with his brother Reginald. He was influenced by his friendship with black women radicals like Queen Mother Audley Moore, a prominent civil rights activist, and Vicki Garvin, a Harlan communist activist.[30] Women also played a crucial role in pushing Malcolm X toward the international stage. Queen Mother Moore was a radical teacher, political organizer, and storyteller.[31] She was a grassroots leader in the Harlem Communist Party until 1950.[32] These broader views also allowed him to shift his understanding of gender politics. As he traveled, he met with women internationally, most of whom were as radical as those with whom he was affiliated at home.

The Nation of Islam (NOI) was a separatist movement, so constructive alterity would seem to have played a pivotal role in the religion—Nation members were "other" than the white culture that surrounded them. Yet, one might also make the argument that Nation women faced the alterity of being singled out by Muhammad for particularly family service to the movement. Since their choices were limited, this could be considered destructive alterity. In this case, men in the movement would not just be defining women as "other," but "lesser." This also made for a layered identity: women were black mothers, and members of the Nation, and teachers or day care workers or caterers.

WOMEN IN NATION OF YAHWEH

The Nation of Yahweh was a movement centered in Miami, Florida, in the 1980s. Hulon Mitchell, Jr., known to his followers as Yahweh ben Yahweh, founded the movement. Mitchell taught a version of Black power and self-help. His community, the Temple of Love in Miami, organized businesses that were entirely staffed by members. They owned restaurants, beauty parlors, apartment complexes, and produced food, health, and beauty products. [33] They encouraged members to support black businesses in an effort to separate themselves from white culture. Mitchell's gender ideology appears to have been patriarchal, in that most leadership positions were filled by men, and some women appear to have been harassed. [34]

Although Yahweh ben Yahweh may have done a lot of charitable work in the Miami area, his group did just as much damage. Eventually, Yahweh ben Yahweh and 12 followers were indicted on charges of racketeering and extortion. As part of the charges, there were 14 killings, two attempted killings, extortion and arson. [35] Members said they were following the teachings of Yahweh ben Yahweh to "kill the white devils," which would bring an age of supremacy for the black community. [36] Only one woman in the movement was originally charged. Judith Israel was described as Yahweh ben Yahweh's deputy. She appears to have been a high-level administrator in the movement. [37]

Men in the Nation of Yahweh (NOY) treated women as "other." According to the prosecuting attorneys, Mitchell used his position of authority to order members to carry out violent actions, to order the killing of defectors, and to force women and girls to be sexually compliant. [38] Mitchell's chosen name, Yahweh ben Yahweh, meant "God, son of God." He understood himself to be the new messiah that would bring about a new age. He taught that God and Jesus were black, which were clear if one understood the Hebrew translations of the scriptures. He taught his followers Hebrew and his interpretation of the scriptures as well. In his book, *Yahweh Judges America,* he describes his scriptural interpretations, and what God wants black people to know about their true Jewish heritage.

His followers wore white, and all buildings bought by the Temple of Love were painted white to distinguish them from other buildings in their neighborhoods. He clearly taught a theology of alterity: he taught that black Hebrews are "other" than white Jews or any other white Americans, for that matter. This was a case of destructive alterity: women and girls were "other," because they could be treated as commodities to be traded or possessed. Women in the movement had to negotiate several identities, including "black," "women," "members of the Nation of Yahweh," among others.

WOMEN IN THE BLACK PANTHER MOVEMENT, PARTICULARLY BPP

While it seems counterintuitive given the group's ultra-masculine and dominant image, the Black Panther Party stands apart from the other Black power
movements in the degree to which it limited destructive intersectional alterity
within its organization. One image that makes this statement powerfully was
taken in 1968 in Oakland's DeFremery Park near a grove of trees honoring
Bobby Hutton. Hutton had been shot at the age of 17 by police, allegedly
trying to surrender and who had been the Panther's first enlisted member. In
the photo, six women at a Free Huey Newton rally stand united, their fists
raised in the BPP salute. Bill Pretzer, the curator of a Smithsonian exhibit
featuring the photograph explains its significance.

> "Women's participation and the issue of gender equality ebbed and flowed
> within the Panthers' history. It didn't simply improve or get larger, or devolve
> and get worse, it goes up and down," he says of the photograph's inclusion. "I
> think at the time and even since, the popular public image of the Black Panther
> Party as a super masculine group of men who were violent and fought the
> authorities pervades public sentiment. This image contradicts that dramatically
> and effectively."[39]

Despite popular perception of the BPP as dominantly masculine, a survey
conducted by Chairman Bobby Seale in 1969 showed that at the apex of the
BPP's influence, the party was more than 60 percent female. Women served
every aspect of the organization, including key leadership roles.[40] Historical
accounts indicate that the first female member was Tarika Lewis, also known
as Matilaba. Lewis asked to join and was told, yes. She then asked for a gun
and was also told, yes.[41]

It must be clearly acknowledged that the influence of strong women in the
BPP evolved over time along with the group's ideological schema. Many
women in the BPP were objectified and suffered unspeakable repercussions
as a result of this alteritous objectification by their male group members. One
particularly heinous example was perpetrated by Eldridge Cleaver, who
joined the BPP as minister of information in 1967. Cleaver explains in his
book, *Soul on Ice*, that he believed that raping white women was a "revolutionary act." He wanted to be sure that he carried out this "revolutionary act"
as efficiently as possible, so he "practiced" on black women in the BPP
before moving on to white victims.[42]

In response to actions like those taken by Eldridge Cleaver, against the
backdrop of the chauvinism of the BPP organization and the American society of the 1960s, the women of the BPP took action. The BPP women saw
their global struggle as one against racism and capitalism as interdependent

oppressive forces, but they saw sexism as something to be addressed within the BPP.[43] Khury Smith explained,

> We had to deal with the issues of chauvinism in the Black Panther Party by having political education classes, and those brothers who didn't want to work under women or were using the "b-word"—those things that cause the deterioration of party—had to be corrected. Because women demanded that. So when those brothers did that and refused to listen to sisters, they were required to take orders from sisters to learn to respect them as their comrades.[44]

The BPP ran "survival programs" to make sure that all people in the black community had their basic needs met so that they had the ability to participate in the political empowerment movement. These survival programs were fundamentally socialist in nature. They were designed to have the community meet the material needs of individuals. Structural and political forces placed women at the vanguard of these programs. The FBI's COINTELPRO campaign led to numerous arrests of male leadership in the BPP, leaving women to lead many organizational initiatives. Women were also closer to the family units socially. Ashley Farmer describes BPP women's role in the survival programs and how that role helped to promote women's leadership across the organization.

Women ran the survival programs both locally and nationally. They were largely responsible for the daily administrative tasks, partnering with other organizations within the community to sustain the programs, and connecting the programs to the Panther's larger political ideology through artwork and articles in The Black Panther newspaper. Survival programs were also one of the main ways the community interacted with the party. When community members saw women confidently running these programs, it bolstered their support for women's leadership in other areas.[45]

The survival programs are just one example of the socialist progression of the BPP. A number of scholars and BPP group members assert that as the organization became more socialist, it also increasingly rejected traditional alteritous male/female power dynamics. When BPP communication secretary Kathleen Cleaver was asked in 1970 what a woman's role was in the revolution, her response was very revealing of the culture reported by women in the organization at the time. She replied, "No one ever asks what a man's place in the Revolution is."[46] Ashley Farmer reflects on the role of socialism in minimizing destructive female alterity in the organization.

> There is a great conversation among a group of Panther women which was transcribed in the Black Panther newspaper that I think encapsulates this point. In the conversation, the women explain that as BPP members became more aware of the inner workings of capitalism and imperialism, they began to better understand how class dynamics influence gender roles. They realized

that traditional gender roles not only restricted their ability to effectively serve their communities, they also fed into capitalist-driven ideas about the family, consumerism, and race.

After coming to this conclusion, they realized that they could not organize against economic oppression without acknowledging the ways in which it specifically affected Black women. Or as they say in the interview, that in a socialist revolution, the emancipation of women is primary. Now, they are certainly borrowing some of these ideas from other discussions of socialism and imperialism at the time. But one of the key points is that the Panthers, and particularly Panther women, were really trying to incorporate gender critiques into their understandings of capitalism, imperialism, and racism in American society.[47]

While socialism is only one of the causes of the BPP's eventual rejection of intersectional destructive alterity, it was a powerful one and it has left a legacy of black female leadership in civil rights causes to this day. Yet, aspects of BPP's experimentation with communal living ended up with men taking advantage of women. While the group interpreted communal living with sexual freedom, what transpired was often sexual exploitation instead.[48] Thus, some destructive alterity took place.

Elaine Brown, a member of the Los Angeles branch of the Black Panthers noted in her biography:

We knew Brothers dragged their old habits into the party. We all did. The party's role, however, was not limited to external revolution but incorporated the revolutionizing of its ranks. If, however, the very leadership of a male-dominated organization was bent on clinging to old habits about women, we had a problem. We would have to fight for the right to fight for freedom.[49]

In the late 1960s, women in the Black Panther Party took party leadership, beginning with the party newspaper. As male leadership in the movement became incarcerated, they were replaced by female members as a practical consideration. This slowly changed the gender dynamics of the movement.

The belief in black male dominance that was antagonistic to "Black womanhood" has remained strong and has shaped scholarly literature on the BPP, despite the rich history of first person accounts written by movement participants and the many books, essay collections and journal articles on women's participation in Black power movements.[50] Yet, women helped lead the BPP into local politics in the 1970s and created a successful organizational structure for everyone to find their roles in the years to come.[51] The BPP thus had periods of progression and regression of alterity; it was an evolving process from which strong female voices emerged.

CONCLUSION

It is undeniable that black women experienced intersectionality in the form of complex layered identities during the civil rights era. Even those women engaged in activist Black power organizations were confronted with the realities of this intersectionality on a daily basis. While organizations promoting black equality and Black power were intentionally conscious of harmful power dynamics that led to destructive racial alterity, they often did not confront destructive gender alterity within their own organizations. An unexpected exception to this was the Black Panther Party as it evolved in the 1970s. As the women of the party acknowledge, different branches of the movement had different environments. There were also many prominent cases of alterity and abuse during the organization's evolution. Overall, however, there was a culture that promoted female leadership and empowerment to a degree not seen in many other Black power movements at the time. We believe that the communitarian/socialist progression of the organization's ideals led to this different approach.

NOTES

1. Imaoboang D. Umoren, "From the Margins to the Center: African American Women's and Gender History since the 1970s," *History Compass* 13/12 (2015): 648.

2. June O. Patton, "African American Women, Civil Rights, and Black power," Essay Review, *Journal of African American History* vol. 89, issue 1 (Summer 2004): 264.

3. Patton, citing Farah Jasmine Griffin and Tracye A. Matthews.

4. Malcolm X, edited by Imam Benjamin Karim. "Black Man's History." Speech Given December, 1962. http://www.malcolm-x.org/speeches/spc_12__62.htm. (accessed August 14, 2012).

5. Wallace, George. Gubernatorial Inaugural Address. January 14, 1963. http://www. archives.alabama.gov/govs_list/inauguralspeech.html (accessed August 16, 2012).

6. *Encyclopedia of Alabama.* "Sixteenth Street Baptist Church." http://www.encyclopedia ofalabama.org/face/Article.jsp?id=h-1744. (accessed August 17, 2012).

7. Kimberlé Crenshaw, "What Is Intersectionality?" National Association of Independent Schools video, published June 22, 2018. Retrieved from https://www.youtube.com/watch?v=ViDtnfQ9FHc

8. Kathryn Kish Sklar and Elaine DeLott Baker, "How and Why Did Women in SNCC (the Student Non-Violent Coordinating Committee) Author a Pathbreaking Feminist Manifesto, 1964–1965?" http://womhist.alexanderstreet.com/SNCC/intro.htm

9. Sklar and Baker.

10. Barbara Ransby, *Ella Baker and the Black Freedom Movement: A Radical Democratic Vision* (Chapel Hill: University of North Carolina Chapel Hill, 2003), 246–47.

11. Ransby, 256.

12. Ransby, 257.

13. Ransby, 292.

14. Ransby, 297.

15. Cynthia S'themble West, "Revisiting Female Activism in the 1960s: The Newark Branch of the Nation of Islam," *The Black Scholar* 26 (Fall 1996/Winter 1997): 3–4; Proquest.

16. Dawn-Marie Gibson, "Nation Women's Engagement and Resistance in the *Muhammad Speaks* Newspaper." *Journal of American Studies* 49 (2015): 1.

17. Gibson, 6.

18. Lauri Umansky, "The Sisters Reply: Black Nationalist Pronatalism, Black Feminism, and the Quest for a Multiracial Women's Movement, 1965–1974," *Critical Matrix* vol. 8, issue 2 (December 31, 1994): 19. Proquest.

19. Umansky, 3.

20. Umansky, 4.

21. Gibson, "Nation Women's Engagement," 6.

22. West, "Revisiting Female Activism," 43.

23. West, 42.

24. West, 45.

25. Gibson, "Nation Women's Engagement," 2.

26. West, "Revisiting Female Activism," 42.

27. Gibson, "Nation Women's Engagement," 8–14.

28. Gibson, 7.

29. Patton, citing Farah Jasmine Griffin and Tracye A. Matthews.

30. Erik McDuffie and Komozi Woodard, "If You're in a Country that's Progressive, the Woman in Progressive:" Black Women Radicals and the Making of Malcolm X," *Biography* 36.3 (Summer 2013): 507–39.

31. McDuffie and Woodard, 522.

32. McDuffie and Woddard, 516.

33. Dawn Hutchinson, *Antiquity and Social Reform: Religious Experience in the Unification Church, Feminist Wicca and Nation of Yahweh* (Newcastle upon Tyne: Cambridge Scholars Publishing, 2010), 125.

34. Associated Press, "Religious Leader Charged in 14 Deaths Yahweh ben Yahweh's Sect Accused of Slayings, Extortion in Federal Charges," *Orlando Sentinel,* November 8, 1980. Proquest.

35. Douglas Martin, "'Wonderful One' Said He Rose from the Dead to Lead a Lost Tribe," *The Globe and Mail*, Toronto, May 11, 2007. Proquest.

36. Jean Dubail and Monica Rohr, "Temple of Love or a Den of Terror?" *Sun Sentinel*, Fort Lauderdale, November 1, 1990. Proquest.

37. "F.B.I. Arrests Members of Black Sect in 14 Slayings," *New York Times*, November 8, 1990, *New York Times* Archives, https://www.nytimes.com/1990/11/08/us/fbi-arrests-members-of-black-sect-in-14-slayings.html

38. Dubail and Rohr, "Temple of Love."

39. Janelle Harris, "The Rank and File Women of the Black Panther Party and Their Powerful Influence," https://www.smithsonianmag.com/smithsonian-institution/rank-and-file-women-black-panther-party-their-powerful-influence-180971591/

40. Robyn C. Spencer, *The Revolution Has Come: Black Power, Gender, and the Black Panther Party in Oakland* (Durham: Duke University Press, 2016), 44.

41. Angela D. LeBlanc-Ernest, "'The Most Qualified Person to Handle the Job': Black Panther Party Women, 1966–1982," in *The Black Panther Party (reconsidered)*, ed. Charles E. Jones (Baltimore: Black Classic Press, 1998), 307–8.

42. Eldridge Cleaver, *Soul on Ice* (New York: McGraw-Hill, 1967), 14.

43. Ashley Farmer, Mary Phillips, Robyn C. Spencer, and Leela Yellesetty, "Women in the Black Panther Party: A Roundtable," *International Socialist Review* issue 111: Interviews.

44. Emory Douglas, "We Always Had Solidarity," interview by Khury Peterson Smith, *Socialist Worker*, May 13, 2015, https://socialistworker.org/2015/05/13/we-always-had-solidarity.

45. Farmer, Phillips, Spencer, and Yellesetty, "Women in the Black Panther Party."

46. Bobby Seale, *A Lonely Rage: The Autobiography of Bobby Seale* (New York: Times Books, 1978), 177.

47. Farmer, Phillips, Spencer, and Yellesetty, "Women in the Black Panther Party."

48. Robyn Ceanne Spencer, "Engendering the Black Freedom Struggle: Revolutionary Black Womanhood and the Black Panther Party in the Bay Area, California," *Journal of Women's History* vol. 20, no. 1 (2008): 91.

49. Elaine Brown, *A Taste of Power: A Black Woman's Story* (New York: Anchor Books, 1991), 191.

50. Spencer, "Engendering the Black Freedom Struggle," 91.
51. Spencer, 91.

REFERENCES

Associated Press. "Religious Leader Charged in 14 Deaths Yahweh ben Yahweh's Sect Accused of Slayings, Extortion in Federal Charges." *Orlando Sentinel*, November 8, 1980. Proquest.

Brown, Elaine. *A Taste of Power: A Black Woman's Story*. New York: Anchor Books, 1991.

Cleaver, Eldridge. *Soul on Ice*. New York: McGraw-Hill, 1967.

Crenshaw, Kimberlé. "What Is Intersectionality?" National Association of Independent Schools video, published June 22, 2018. Retrieved from https://www.youtube.com/watch?v=ViDtnfQ9FHc

Douglas, Emory. "We Always Had Solidarity." interview by Khury Peterson Smith, *Socialist Worker*, May 13, 2015, https://socialistworker.org/2015/05/13/we-always-had-solidarity.

Dubail, Jean, and Monica Rohr. "Temple of Love or a Den of Terror?" *Sun Sentinel*, Fort Lauderdale, November 1, 1990. Proquest.

Encyclopedia of Alabama. "Sixteenth Street Baptist Church." http://www.encyclopedia ofalabama.org/face/Article.jsp?id=h-1744. (accessed August 17, 2012).

Farmer, Ashley, Mary Phillips, Robyn C. Spencer, and Leela Yellesetty. "Women in the Black Panther Party: A Roundtable." *International Socialist Review* issue 111: Interviews.

Gibson, Dawn-Marie. "Nation Women's Engagement and Resistance in the *Muhammad Speaks* Newspaper." *Journal of American Studies* 49 (2015): 1–18.

Harris, Janelle. "The Rank and File Women of the Black Panther Party and Their Powerful Influence." https://www.smithsonianmag.com/smithsonian-institution/ rank-and-file-women-black-panther-party-their-powerful-influence-180971591/

Hutchinson, Dawn. *Antiquity and Social Reform: Religious Experience in the Unification Church, Feminist Wicca and Nation of Yahweh* (Newcastle upon Tyne: Cambridge Scholars Publishing, 2010).

Karim, Imam Benjamin, ed. *Malcolm X, "Black Man's History."* Speech Given December, 1962. http://www.malcolm-x.org/speeches/spc_12__62.htm. (accessed August 14, 2012).

LeBlanc-Ernest, Angela D. "'The Most Qualified Person to Handle the Job': Black Panther Party Women, 1966–1982," in *The Black Panther Party (reconsidered)*, ed. Charles E. Jones. Baltimore: Black Classic Press, 1998.

Martin, Douglas. "'Wonderful One' Said He Rose from the Dead to Lead a Lost Tribe." *The Globe and Mail*, Toronto, May 11, 2007. Proquest.

McDuffie, Erik, and Komozi Woodard. "'If You're in a Country that's Progressive, the Woman Is Progressive': Black Women Radicals and the Making of Malcolm X." *Biography* 36.3 (Summer 2013).

Patton, June O. "African American Women, Civil Rights, and Black Power." Essay Review, *Journal of African American History* vol. 89, issue 1 (Summer 2004): 262–65.

Ransby, Barbara. *Ella Baker and the Black Freedom Movement: A Radical Democratic Vision*. Chapel Hill: University of North Carolina Chapel Hill, 2003.

Sklar, Kathryn Kish, and Elaine DeLott Baker. "How and Why Did Women in SNCC (the Student Non-Violent Coordinating Committee) Author a Pathbreaking Feminist Manifesto, 1964–1965?" http://womhist.alexanderstreet.com/SNCC/intro.htm

Seale, Bobby. *A Lonely Rage: The Autobiography of Bobby Seale*. New York: Times Books, 1978.

Spencer, Robyn Ceanne. "Engendering the Black Freedom Struggle: Revolutionary Black Womanhood and the Black Panther Party in the Bay Area, California." *Journal of Women's History* vol. 20, no. 1 (2008).

Spencer, Robyn C. *The Revolution Has Come: Black Power, Gender, and the Black Panther Party in Oakland*. Durham: Duke University Press, 2016.

Umansky, Lauri. "The Sisters Reply": Black Nationalist Pronatalism, Black Feminism, and the Quest for a Multiracial Women's Movement, 1965–1974." *Critical Matrix* vol. 8, issue 2 (December 31, 1994): 19. Proquest.

Umoren, Imaoboang D. "From the Margins to the Center: African American Women's and Gender History since the 1970s." *History Compass* 13/12 (2015): 646–58.

Wallace, George. Gubernatorial Inaugural Address. January 14, 1963. http://www.archives.alabama.gov/govs_list/inauguralspeech.html (accessed August 16, 2012).

West, Cynthia S'themble. "Revisiting Female Activism in the 1960s: The Newark Branch of the Nation of Islam." *The Black Scholar*, Fall 1996/Winter 1997.

Chapter Two

Poverty and the Challenges of Women's Participation in Nigerian Politics

Gaius Jatau

In Nigeria, the question of gender, power, and rights, economic and reproductive rights of women have come to the fore; those gender gaps are wide-
spread in rights, access to, and control of resources in economic opportunities and political participation. Lack of resources and economic opportunities of women either at the corridor of power or not, increases women's
poverty; this constitutes a challenge to their participation in politics. Gender
disparities constrain the set of choices available to women in many aspects of
life; especially, limiting their ability to participate in, and benefitting from
politics or political development.[1] More so, the difference in gender and
political power is explicable in terms of the different social structures; such
as culture, education, religion, poverty, and discrimination, amongst others.
These social structures in nineteenth-century Nigeria had developed through
systematic historical events, and were undergoing considerable internal and
external changes, especially, from the mid-century. Some of these changes
and events provided opportunities for some women to play a greater role in
politics.

In the real sense, Nigerian politics is male-dominated and women are not
treated as equal partners politically, despite the numerous international in-
struments/charters and constitutional provisions affirming the equality of
men and women in all spheres of life. Women in Nigeria have, like in most
countries of the world, the two most fundamental democratic rights: the right
to vote and the right to stand for election to be voted. However, because of
poverty, women who intend to engage in politics have been constrained.

The cultural theory posits that patriarchy is the process whereby societal powers generally rest with men and the various structures of the society consistently assign inferior or secondary roles to women, and other cultural indices perpetuate fundamental inequality.[2] This is the case in Nigeria, in affirmation to this theory: the place of women in politics is not equal to that of men. This could be a result of cultural differences, and the level of poverty amongst others that have rendered women poorer than men. Furthermore, the theory being a social system in which men dominate the polity posits that men largely dominate the political sphere, and largely formulate the rules of the political game. Political life is organized according to male norms and values, and in some cases even male lifestyles. This may often result in women either rejecting politics altogether or rejecting male-style politics. Thus, when women do participate in politics, they tend to do so in small numbers.[3]

The theory helps to describe and interprets existing phenomenon. It attempts to investigate, establish, and explain the factors behind the underrepresentation of women at all levels of power and leadership and to set the pace for better and enhanced women's political participation through effective ways. This study on women's participation in politics and governance could make a valuable contribution to more general theories of democratic process. Therefore, the study adopts the notion of the cultural theory on patriarchy to serve as lens to understand the participation of women in politics.

WOMEN'S PARTICIPATION IN NIGERIAN POLITICS

The marginal participation of women in party politics has made it difficult for visible women party constituencies to emerge or develop. Between 1957 and 1959, there were four major political parties in Nigeria: Northern Peoples' Congress (NPC), National Council of Nigerian Citizens (NCNC), Northern Elements Progressive Union (NEPU), and Action Group (AG). In the executive bodies of these political parties, men dominated while women were almost invisible. It was only NEPU that had a woman on its national executive board designated as women's organizer.[4]

Since the emergence of indigenous political leadership in 1960, Nigerian women have remained insignificant in politics. Women were grossly underrepresented in party membership as well as in decision-making fora. In the legislative assemblies where laws governing the nation were made, women were underrepresented. For instance, between 1960 and 1966, there were only two women in the Senate, the highest decision law making body. In the 1980s out of 95 senators, only 1 was a woman, while in the lower parliament, out of 445 parliamentarians, only 3 were women. Also, in the same period, men largely dominated the National Executive Councils of the parties. Out of

35 members that constituted the National Executive Councils, only 4 were women.[5]

Again, under the Second Republic, 1979–1983, in the Senate elections, out of 479 contestants, only 4 were women. In the Federal House of Representatives elections, out of the 2,000 candidates presented by the different political parties, only 10 were women. Similarly, in the Third Republic, out of 330 governorship aspirants, only 9 were women and surprisingly, none won from their party nomination.[6] From all indications, women were not adequately represented here. Although the number of women participating in politics from the Fourth Republic increased gradually, it is still not adequate.

It is interesting to mention that a few women have occupied important key administrative and political positions since 1999. In most instances, these women have performed creditably well, thereby leaving no doubt about the ability and capability of women to perform when saddled with responsibilities at all levels. Despite the challenges of poverty in Nigeria, women have contested under various party platforms for different positions in the five general elections held between 1999 and 2015. However, women's participation recorded poor results, minimal gains and slow progress. For example, in 2003, women made up only 3 percent of elected officials, in 2007, they made up 7 percent, and in 2011 they made about 5 percent and before the 2015 general elections few women emerged as candidates after the primaries of the various political parties.[7] In 2015, gubernatorial elections were held. In 29 states, the representation of women who contested for the office of governor and deputy governor was 87 out of the 380 candidates, and this represents 22.9 percent. For the senatorial seats, 122 women out of 747 candidates, this represents 16 percent, of those cleared by the Independent National Electoral Commission (INEC) to run in the election. Worst of all, was the contest for House of Representatives, out of 1774 candidates that ran for the seats, 267 were women representing 15 percent.[8]

Using mega parties to analyze women's participation in politics in 2015, one argues that the Progressive People's Party (PPP) had the highest number of women who contested seats in the House of Representatives and 16 for senate. Labour Party had 15 for House of Representatives and 7 for senate. The People's Democratic Party (PDP) had 19 women for the House of Representatives and 7 for senate, while the All Progressives Congress (APC) had 26 women for the House of Representatives and 7 for the senate. All these together with other mini-parties, put women contestants below 35 percent.[9]

Comparison of Women's Representation in the Nigerian Elections: 1999, 2003, 2007, and 2011

	1999 Seats Available	Women	2003 Seats Available	Women	2007 Seats Available	Women	2011 Seats Available
	1	0	1	0	1	0	1
	109	3 (2.8%)	109	4 (3.7%)	109	9 (8.3%)	109
s	360	12 (3.3%)	360	21 (5.8%)	360	25 (6.9%)	360
	36	0	36	0	36	0	36
	990	24 (2.4%)	990	40 (3.9%)	990	57 (5.8%)	990
	829	18 (2.2%)	881	32 (3.6%)	887	52 (5.9%)	887
ea	710	13 (1.8%)	774	15 (1.9%)	740	27 (3.6%)	740
	6368	69 (1.1%)	6368	267 (4.2%)	6368	235 (3.7%)	6368

d from Ugwuegede Patience Nwabunkeonye "Challenges to Women Active Participation in Politics in Niger www.hrpub.org. *Time*, November 20, 2018. Also Independent National Electoral Commission (INEC) Of , December 4, 2018.

In all the 36 states in Nigeria, since the inception of democracy in 1999 up to 2015, there has not been a female governor, and the country is not ready to have a woman as president. Yet, a woman contested for the post of a president in 2015, but did not win. These are basic realities on ground, despite the National Gender Policy promise to support women to occupy 35 percent of elective positions in Nigeria. More so, development experts and gender activists have continuously advocated for the active participation of women in governance for the good of society. But in the 2015 general elections, the situation remained unimproved in the country.[10] To sum up this analysis, the tables below provide tabular figures of women participating in politics between 1999 and 2011.

Table 2.1 provides a sample of available seats and the number of women that contested for those seats from 1999, 2003, 2007, and 2011 General elections. From 1999 to 2011 under the president and governor, there was no female aspirant. In the Senate, House of Representatives and State House of Assemblies, there was an increase in the percentage of female representation. However in 2011, there was no women representation in the State House of Assembly Committee, Local Government Area Chairperson, and Councillors. This is a clear indication that of all the elective seats into the various categories indicated above, men dominated the representation.

Table 2.2. The Statistics of Nigerian Women in Political Participation and Performance from 1999–2015

S/N	Position	Seats	Women				
			1999	2003	2007	2011	2015
1	Presidency	2	0	0	0	0	0
2	Senate	109	3	4	8	7	8
3	House of Reps	360	12	23	26	26	14
4	Governorship	36	0	0	0	0	0
5	Deputy Governorship	36	1	2	6	3	4
6	State House of Assemblies	990	12	38	54	62	—
7	**Total**	**1533**	**28**	**67**	**94**	**98**	**26**

Source: Adapted from Abdullahi Mohammed Abdul, Muhammad Bello and Aminu Ibrahim, "Cultural Beliefs and the Challenges of Women Participation in Nigerian Politics," *Kaduna Journal of Historical Studies,* vol. 9, no. 2 (2017): 355.

Table 2.2 provides the statistics of Nigerian women participation and performance in politics in 1999, 2003, 2007, 2011, and 2015, respectively. At the presidency, there was no women representation while there was women representation in the rest of the positions, which kept increasing since 1999, except in 2015, when there was no representation in the State House of Assemblies. The fact remains that women are grossly underrepresented in the legislative and executive arms of government and are being short-changed in the political activities in Nigeria. Women activists and groups in Nigeria had since 1995, been advocating for an increase in the number of women in political positions, however, little has been achieved. The representation of men and women in elected positions in 2015 as shown in table below is a clear affirmation to such claims.

Table 2.3 shows the number of men and women in elected positions in the general elections of 2015. Out of the various elective positions, there were 517 men, while there were 26 women. This is quite inadequate giving that the 2015 general elections did not deviate from the pattern of the previous elections, and women were optimistic that their aspirations in the political process would receive a boost from the level of preparations undertaken in that direction.

Although women have been playing a crucial role in Nigerian politics, their participation has remained insignificant compared to the role of men and their participation in politics. Even though women are participating in politics at higher rates than before, they are faced with different challenges such as poverty, culture, discrimination, marriage, and domestic work. This paper examines among these challenges, poverty and women's participation in the politics of Nigeria.

Table 2.3.   The Representation of Men and Women in Elective Positions in 2015

S/N	Position	Men	Women	Total
1	President	1	0	1
2	Vice President	1	0	1
3	Senate	101	8	109
4	House of Representatives	346	14	360
5	Governor	36	0	36
6	Deputy Governor	32	4	36
7	House of Assembly	—	—	990
		517	**26**	**1533**

Source: Independent National Electoral Commission (INEC) Office UnguwanRimi, Kaduna, Nigeria. December 4, 2018.

THE INFLUENCE OF POVERTY ON WOMEN'S PARTICIPATION IN NIGERIAN POLITICS

The feminization of poverty and lack of financial resources over the years constituted the problem of women's participation in Nigerian politics. This has been so given the low participation in the various Republics in Nigeria since 1999. For example, from the tables discussed above, Nigeria witnessed a sharp influence in terms of women's participation in politics. The turn-around has created a new awareness that women should have a responsibility to participate in the affairs of Nigerian society. The increase of women's participation in politics was also witnessed during the 2015 General Elections. The election produced a woman presidential aspirant in the person of Professor Oluremi Sonaya, and Senator Aisha Jumai Al-Hassan for governorship election.[11] The participation and appointments of women in these republics have contributed in some measures to the socioeconomic and political development of Nigeria.

Despite the significant advances in women's achievements in education, work, and other sectors of public life, politically, women remain a minority in Nigerian politics. The poor representation and participation of Nigerian women at the higher levels of political activity, and decision-making since the return to civil rule in 1999 is attributed to several factors, like; poverty, culture, marriage, marginalization/discrimination, and education. For example, women are often marginalized or excluded at the crucial levels of party formation. Men dominate the political party structure, design the party constitution, and formulate other unwritten rules that guide the party, and at best crown the women with "woman leader" or an "ex-officio" of a women's wing.[12] Women's marginalization and discrimination in politics result to women participation and representation in politics, which has implications for women's psychological imbalance and continue to hinder their contributions to political development.

Crucial to all these challenges is poverty, which is the main crux of this paper. The increased level of poverty in Nigeria affects women's participation in politics. Lack of finances is a serious hindrance to effective women's participation in Nigerian politics and political development of Nigeria. Due to poverty, women are not financially capable as their men counterparts to deeply engage in active politics as the men do because of their financial capabilities. Significantly, the numbers of Nigerians living in poverty are on the increase, poverty rates remain high in Nigeria, particularly in rural areas where women constitute 70 percent. Even though these rates declined between 2003–2004 and 2009–2010, respectively, it was slow, not as fast as expected from the pace of economic growth in the country.[13] The United Nations statistics shows that out of 1.3 billion people living in poverty around the world, 70 percent are women. Women work two-thirds of the world's working hours, produced half of the world's food and yet earn only 10 percent of the world's income and own less than 1 percent of the world's property. [14]

In Nigeria, there are a number of civil society organizations on gender issues, and a number of top women political appointees ranging from Supreme Court judges, ministers, deputy governors, director-generals, and permanent secretaries up to ambassadors, but poverty still remains a challenge for women. This crucial challenge of poverty affects their participation in politics, because politics in Nigeria is a game of money. Money is required for registration with a party of interest for ward counsellor, chairman, State House of Assembly, House of Representatives, Senate, and President. From all indications, money determines one's majority votes in Nigerian politics, even if it should not. The involvement of money in the political process by the state and the political class is a major impediment to women's participation in politics and governance. Nigerian politics is money, and money is Nigerian politics. For instance, available evidence shows that monetization of the political process during the Second and Third Republics served as a disincentive to the participation of women in contesting for elective offices in the then existing political parties as well as executive and legislative positions. This was glaring in the Third Republic during the President Ibrahim Badamasi Babangida's transition program; the cost of nomination for elective positions was high. Presidential aspirants under the Social Democratic Party (SDP) paid a non-refundable nomination fee of N500,000 each, while the National Republican Convention (NRC) aspirants paid N400,000 each. Out of the 31 aspirants for the parties' primaries, only 19 eventually contested and none were women. The 3 women presidential aspirants on the platform of SDP in person of Sarah Jubril, Maria Braimah and Catherine Wayas, could not fulfil the financial requirements of the party. [15]

Financial requirements for contesting party tickets, mobilization of voters and planned campaigns were a major setback for potential contestants, most especially women. In the Third Republic, it was estimated that to fund a presidential primary, an aspirant must have between N300 and N400 million, which was beyond the reach of all the women presidential aspirants. To exemplify the poor financial situation of the women politicians was the case of Sarah Jubril, who in her campaign mobilization went about campaigning in hired taxicabs in areas outside Lagos State. While in Lagos State, she transported herself in rickety yellow buses known as "molue," while her male counterparts, who were financially buoyant, were able to mobilize voters across the country conveniently. In addition, campaign offices of these male contestants were visibly located in all the Nigerian states, and their campaign components such as vehicle, transportation, poster, handbills, radio, and television advertisements were conveniently financed. [16]

Politics in Nigeria, especially seeking elected positions is an expensive venture that requires a huge financial involvement. More so, the relatively poor financial position of Nigerian women is a critical challenge that mostly accounts for their low participation in politics. About 90 percent of women in Nigeria currently live below the poverty line.[17] Some major political parties lowered the cost of obtaining party nomination forms for women into elective office, but still the money to buy the forms were far beyond the reach of even the most highly placed women who do not have sponsors. Most importantly, looking at the financial position, and lack of godfathers' and other financiers of politicians in Nigeria, the male political aspirants are preferred than the female ones, based on the societal value assumption that political activities are masculine, and male candidates are believed to stand better chance of winning elections. In Nigeria, women have less access to credit facilities, lack of control of their income and resources, while living with their husbands contributes to their lack of financial strength, which is a major challenge in their active participation in politics.[18]

The financial demand for contesting any political position in Nigeria is high, to the extent that women, no matter how highly placed they are in the society, cannot afford to buy nomination forms even if interested. This paper uses two popular political parties, the All Progressive Congress (APC) and the People's Democratic Party (PDP) as example in the general elections of 2019. Tables 2.4 and 2.5 are here presented to illustrate nomination fees by aspirants in different categories of interests in the various elective posts.

Table 2.4 shows the APC expression of interest and nomination fees put together of the Presidential, Governor, Senatorial, House of Representatives, and State House of Assemblies. The amount differs and is based on the category or position. The highest amount is that of the president, while the lowest amount on the list is that of the State House of Assemblies.

Table 2.4.   The All Progressive Congress (APC) Nomination Fees into Elective Posts for 2019 General Elections

S/N	Category	Expression of Interest	Nomination	Total
1	Presidential	N5m	N40m	N45m
2	Governor	N2.5m	N20m	N22.5m
3	Senatorial	N1m	N6m	N7m
4	House of Reps	N350,000	N3.5m	N3.85m
5	State House of Assemblies	N100,000	N750,000	N850,000

Source: Otitolaye Samuel, Home/Politics/2019 Elections: See the cost of APC forms, published online September 6, 2018.

Table 2.5 graphically illustrates the PDP expression of interest and nomination fees from the presidential office to the 3 ad-hoc delegates. The highest amount paid in this category is the president, followed by the governorship position. The lowest paid are the 3 ad-hoc delegates that paid N5,000, compared to the presidential that paid N12 million.

Considering the money involvement in Nigerian politics, one might wonder how women would get money to actively be involved. Well-financed men might not be willing to sponsor women who have interests in politics but don't have money. From all indications, Nigerian politics is money; money is Nigerian politics; money is the absence of poverty, and poverty is the absence of money. Therefore, politics without money may attract crowds of women into politics. More so, eradicating poverty will have a positive impact on women's increased participation in the democratic process. Therefore, it follows that the economic empowerment of women would take women to full participation in politics and political elections.

CONCLUSION

The role of women in the socioeconomic and political development of Nigeria can help balance the polity. Even though traditionally, and almost universally, women are associated with the home and men with the public task, the indispensability of women in politics is not fiction, but an undoubtable fact. The early human society started with women and they have their relevant roles, even in the present day. The challenges of women's contribution to political development in Nigeria have a downturn in the performance of women, most especially since the return to civil rule in 1999. Although

Table 2.5. The Peoples' Democratic Party (PDP) Nomination Fees into Elective Posts for 2019 General Elections

S/N	Category	Expression of Interest	Nomination	Total
1	Presidential	N2m	N10m	N12m
2	Governorship	N1m	N5m	N6m
3	Senate	N500,000	N3m	N3.5m
4	House of Reps	N500,000	N1m	N1.5m
5	State House of Assembly	N500,000	N500,000	N600,000
6	National Delegate	—	N20,000	N20,000
7	3 Ad-hoc Delegate	—	N5,000	N5,000

Source: PDP National Secretariat, Abuja, 2018.

women have proved their worth in the professional appointments into various political and none political offices, they could still advance politically, if adequate economic empowerment is provided.

In order to empower more women to participate in politics and contribute their quota to political development in Nigeria like their men counterparts, they need support. Women need to be invited to participate in various economic programs and businesses that will improve their financial status. Women should be given equal access to credit facilities and factors of production like land and labor just like men to enhance their output and income generation. Family members should give female political aspirants the relevant consent and support to venture into politics and governance, through financial support, awareness campaign and voters' education programs. Women should be informed of their political rights to participate actively in politics not only as voters but also as candidates, in the numerous political positions, and be encouraged to support and vote for their fellow women political aspirants or politicians. Even though there is poverty, and it has affected women's participation in politics, women have proved their worth in the professional and appointive positions in Nigeria, but this could still be improved upon with adequate economic empowerment to enable them access to finances, and other aspect of socio-political life.

NOTES

1. Titilope Olusegun Olalere, "Women and Development: The Politics of Seclusion in Nigeria," *Kaduna Journal of Historical Studies,* vol. 9, no. 2, (2017): 419.

2. Abdullahi Mohammed Abdul, Bello Baban Umma Muhammad, and Aminu Ibrahim, "Cultural Beliefs and the Challenges of Women Participation in Nigerian Politics." *Kaduna Journal of Historical Studies,* vol. 9, no. 2, (2017): 349–50.

3. Abdul, Muhammad, and Ibrahim, *Kaduna Journal of Historical Studies,* 350.

4. Terhemba Wuam, Boumo Ezonbi, and Changwak E. Jonah, eds., *The Fourth Republic in Nigeria,* (Lagos: Bahiti and Dalila, 2017), 149–50.

5. Wuam, Ezonbi, and Jonah, *Fourth Republic,*151.

6. Wuam, Ezonbi, and Jonah, 151.

7. Abdul, Muhammad, and Ibrahim, *Kaduna Journal of Historical Studies,* 351.

8. Abdul, Muhammad, and Ibrahim, 351.

9. Abdul, Muhammad, and Ibrahim, 353.

10. Adesuwa Tsan, "2015 Elections: How Women Fared." Leadership Newspaper, April 17, 2018.

11. Olalere, "Women and Development," 428.

12. Olalere, 429.

13. Olalere, 430, also, World Bank Economic Report, May 2013.

14. Olalere, 430, also, United Nations Human Development Index, 2013.

15. Wuam, Ezonbi, and Jonah, *Fourth Republic,* 154.

16. Wuam, Ezonbi, and Jonah, 155.

17. Christopher O. Ngara, and Aybam, A. T. "Women in Politics and Decision-making in Nigeria: Challenges and Prospects," *European Journals of Business and Social Sciences,* 2(8): 47–58.

18. Ugwuegede Patience Nwabunkeonye "Challenges to Women Active Participation in Politics in Nigeria," *Time*, November 20, 2018. DOI: 10.13189/sa.2014.020704. www.hrpub.org.

REFERENCES

Abdul, Abdullahi Mohammed, Bello Baban Umma Muhammad, and Aminu Ibrahim. 2017. "Cultural Beliefs and the Changes and the Challenges of Women Participation in Nigerian Politics." *Kaduna Journal of Historical Studies* 348–63.

Irabor, F. O. *Review of Women's Participation and Performance at the 2011 General Elections in Nigeria.* Accessed November 23, 2018. www.baobwomen.org.

Ngara, O. Christopher, and A. T. Ayabam. 2013. "Women and Politics and Decision Making in Nigeria: Challenges and Prospects." *European Journals of Business and Social Sciences* 2(8): 47–58.

Nwabunkeonye, Patience Ugwuegede. 2018. *Challenges to Women Active Participation in Politics in Nigeria.* November. Accessed December 20, 2018. www.hrpub.org.

Olalere, Titilope Olusegun. 2017. "Women and Development: The Politics of Seclusion in Nigeria." *Kaduna Journal of Historical Studies*, vol. 9, no. 2, 418–35.

Otitolaye, Samuel, *Home/Politics/2019 Elections: see the cost of APC Forms*, Published Online September 6, 2019.

Tsan, Adesuwa. "2015 Elections: How Women Fared." *Leadership* newspaper, April 17, 2018.

Udodinma, Okoronko-Chukwu. 2011. "Female Representation in Nigeria: The Case of 2011 General Elections and the Falacy of 35 percent Affirmative Action." *Research on Humanities and Social Sciences* 3(2): 39–46.

Wuam, Terhemba, Ezonbi Boumo, and Changwak E. Jonah. 2017. *The Fourth Republic in Nigeria.* Lagos: Bahiti and Dalila.

Chapter Three

Her Evolution from Terrorized Victim to Psycho-kinetic Madwoman

A Survey of Gothic Heroines

Jason Ray Carney

The Gothic is a category of feminist activist literature, art, and film that delivers its aesthetic effect through a two-part process of dramatically staged uncreation or "de-reification,"[1] by which the "ordinary" or dominant patriarchal order is troubled and exposed as historically contingent: first, the Gothic work establishes an effect of reality and then, second, it stages convincing violations of this effect of reality.

In terms of literary history, the Gothic's origin is in the sensationalistic novels of the late eighteenth and early nineteenth centuries that featured haunted castles, manipulative priests, and other fictionalized residues of feudalism and absolutism often originating from Southern Europe.[2] These scarecrow medievalisms were uniquely spine-tingling from the perspective of the typical Anglophone novel reader of the period, most likely bourgeois, Protestant, and female.[3] Is it surprising that, in addition to the central tropes listed above, the Gothic always features a terrorized female heroine blessed (or cursed) with keen sensitivity and perceptual acuity? Indeed, such a surrogate compellingly allegorizes the female reader of feminist activist literature and even suggests her actual world beyond the unreal real one rendered in ink on leaves and bound in boards.

BRIEF LITERARY HISTORY OF THE GOTHIC

Horace Walpole's *The Castle of Otranto* (1764) is often framed by literary historians as the first Gothic novel; moreover, it is the model that that inspired a cascade of enduring and ephemeral imitators. Published in 1764, *Otranto* tells the story of Manfred, the last lord of the Castle of Otranto, whose profligate aristocratic privilege leads him to force the betrothal of the young, innocent, and virginal protagonist, Isabella. The novel's labyrinthine plot is legendary. Layered among several subplots of intergenerational sin and mystery are supernatural occurrences and hauntings that have become the stock supernatural spectacles of the Gothic literary tradition: moldy dungeons, spectral knights, sighing and animated paintings, trap doors that open and close autonomously, clanking chains, and skeletons. Indeed, with this novel, Walpole would establish as the Gothic's key distinctive features: its readiness to establish a literary effect of reality, its rendering of the supernatural, and, most importantly, its exclusive reliance on a terrorized female protagonist marked by her sensorium, one powerful enough to pierce the veil.

The supernaturalisms of the Gothic were not new in literary history. Gothic fictions' scandalous violation of the literary effect of reality should not distract us from remembering that the foundation upon with Gothic fiction relies, Literary Realism, had once been innovative and that it had been developed only a few decades prior to Walpole.[4] The literary style known as Realism, a narrative rhetoric associated with early eighteenth-century novelists—e.g., Daniel Defoe, Samuel Richardson, and Henry Fielding (in the Anglophone world)—provided writers with models and conventions for formally establishing a literary effect of reality. The reality effect formally rendered by the literary realists seemed to require not only attentive focus on the mundane in a quasi-journalistic fashion but also the eschewal of the supernatural and the tropes of medieval sentimentality characteristic of a previous literary movement: Romance. From the perspective of the Literary Realism that preceded it, the Gothic novel of Walpole represents less a late eighteenth-century innovation and more a return to the themes and formal devices of an earlier Romance tradition, a modulated Romance that incorporates the formal innovations of Realism and that emphasizes fear and a female protagonist.

To what extent is the Gothic truly innovative or instead a resurgence of the cultural compulsions that manifested previously as Romance? This is a question for another time. And yet, initial comparisons between the Romance and the Gothic tradition reveal surprising differences, the most salient being (1) the Gothic, unlike the Romance, is meant to inspire not wonder but terror[5] and, (2) the Gothic tale, unlike the Romance, has a female rather than a male protagonist. Whereas both the Romance and the Gothic are similar in their truck with the supernatural and their deploying of quasi-medieval tropes—settings, costume, character archetypes, etc.—they are different in their emotional inflection and gender dynamics, i.e., wonder (Romance) over fear (Gothic), male protagonist (Romance) over female protagonist (Gothic).

Seen in this way, the Gothic novel differs from the Romance in its emphasis on a modern female heroine imperiled, accordingly, by quasi-medieval threats: in the Romance, a confident male questing knight ventures into the unknown and slays a variety of enemies and monsters, often for the sake of a woman-as-prize, a damsel in distress; accordingly, in the Gothic, the damsel in distress is transformed into the protagonist and she is often beset by threats that take the form of quasi-medieval entities: knights, monks, nuns, ghosts, devils, demons, and haunted castles frighten and disorient her throughout. In short, the Gothic is an ideological inversion of the Romance.

From a literary historical perspective, a genealogy of the Gothic that takes into consideration the extent to which it is influenced by both Romance and Realism must view the gender dynamics of the protagonist as of fundamental significance. Juxtaposed against the adventuring quester of Romance, the anxious and terrorized female protagonist of the Gothic reveals a cultural logic at play of wide-ranging significance. The rest of this essay will explore the significance of this shift by considering the distinctiveness of select female Gothic protagonists and heroines.

THE CASTLE OF OTRANTO AND ISABELLA

Walpole's character of Isabella is arguably the first Gothic heroine. She represents an archetype that later Gothic heroines are defined against. Isabella finds herself in a threatening medieval labyrinth that is peopled by men and supernatural entities of ill-intention. And, most importantly, she is defined by her intense perceptual acuity, her access to the supernatural. There is a thematic logic at play in Gothic narratives that links the female protagonists' perceptual access to the supernatural with her incarceration in a labyrinth, castle, or decaying mansion and her being threatened by a male protagonist; it is only when the female protagonist is incarcerated and threatened that her radical perceptual power pierces the very reality principle established by the writer. In addition to her incarceration in a threatening labyrinth, it is her powerful sensorium that characterizes the Gothic heroine, a sensorium capable of seeing through and beyond the virtual reality principle established in the novel.

Unfortunately, Walpole's novel does not render Isabella as a dynamic or psychologically complex character. She serves as a neutral, often passive surrogate for the reader to identify with, a virtual sensorium for the reader to adopt for accessing supernatural spectacles themselves. But this original

Gothic heroine epitomized by Isabella would be developed into a more dynamic character by a later Gothic novelist: Anne Radcliffe.

THE MYSTERIES OF ULDOLPHO AND EMILY ST. AUBERT

Anne Radcliffe (1764–1823) is considered a master of the Gothic novel and her *The Mysteries of Uldolpho* is arguably the greatest literary achievement of the Gothic flowering of the 1780s and 1790s. The supernatural occurrences depicted by Walpole were not domesticated for the reader, and because of this the Gothic novel tradition he initiated suffered losses to its reputation, for it offended against dominant bourgeoisie views of the supernatural. Belief in the supernatural was seen by the late eighteenth-century Anglophone bourgeoisie reading class as indicative of lower class origins and therefore, by way of class prejudices, its depiction was understood as an aesthetic flaw; however, Radcliffe sought to restore aesthetic dignity to Gothic literary enterprise Walpole inspired, and she did this by explaining away the supernatural occurrences she rendered in her novels in materialist terms. Ghosts, haunted paintings, spectral music: these were pranks, misunderstandings, the result of serendipitous circumstances. These circumstances only gave the appearance of the supernatural. And yet, like Walpole, Radcliffe centered her Gothic novels around terrorized female protagonists who are distinguished by their powerful sensoriums and their consequent perceptual access to the supernatural, irrespective of whether it was explained away or not in the end.

Consider Radcliffe's most celebrated protagonist, Emily St. Aubert, the focus character of *The Mysteries of Udolpho* (1792). Emily's unique power comes from her powerful sensorium, her acute sensitivity. She is a musician, artist, and poet. She is also spiritually-sensitive and devoted, praying often and feeling empathy for everything and everyone, from her family to animals to the very antagonists who threaten her. She is framed in the novel as intensively perceptive, and her perceptual acumen gives her access to supernatural phenomena: ghosts, spectral music, haunted paintings, and other strange phenomena. In the world of the novel, Emily's sensitiveness is both her strength and a source of her aesthetic potential as a protagonist. To the extent that the supernatural phenomena of the novel are focalized through Emily's point of view, they are intensified for the reader. Emily rarely takes action in response to threats, however. A shortcoming of Radcliffe's novels is that the female protagonist, while central to the narrative, serves as only a victim to the intense spectacles to which she is extremely sensitive. Bad things happen to Emily. She witnesses marvels. But it is only through the luck of the benevolence of male saviors that she is whisked away into a place of safety.

THE MONK AND ANTONIA

By juxtaposing Radcliffe's and Walpole's protagonists we see the Gothic is a literature that focuses on the terrorizing of acutely sensitive women who possess sensorium of extreme power that are both sources of joy and terror.[5] This convention is reproduced by a later Gothic novelist who responds directly to Radcliffe: Matthew Gregory Lewis. Lewis' late Gothic novel, *The Monk* (1796), tells the story of Brother Ambrosio and his illicit lust for the young Antonia. In typical Gothic fashion the novel's plot of maze-like, incorporating several subplots and minor characters, but the central story is the descent into sinfulness undertaken by Brother Ambrosio and the terrorizing and eventual torture of the innocent Antonia who, like previous Gothic heroines, is incarcerated in an underground labyrinth and terrorized by supernatural imagery. Antonia, like Radcliffe's Isabella, shows how the function of the female protagonist in the Gothic is to be a sensitive sensorium to terrorize; accordingly, through reading the novel, the reader partakes in the strange pleasure of experience, via the protagonist, this terror. Most importantly, this Gothic heroine appears to have no or little agency.

NINETEENTH-CENTURY GOTHIC

The history of the Gothic after its effulgence in the 1780s and 1790s becomes more difficult to track; this is because, arguably, after the 1790s, as a result of Radcliffe's and several of her imitators success, the conventionalized Gothic went out of fashion. This is not to say the Gothic, as a distinctive cultural/ aesthetic logic, disappeared. To the contrary, several authors reproduced its tropes and echoed its conventions in surprising ways in several diversifying forms; for example, Jane Austen's *Northanger Abbey* is clearly a parody of the Gothic novel that had become overly conventionalized. Although the conventional Gothic novel might have disappeared after 1790, its legacy continued in the form of an evolving Gothic heroine who, unlike their progenitors, used their distinctive sensitivity and perceptual acumen to claim agency. For example, consider the eponymous protagonist of Charlotte Brontë's *Jane Eyre* (1847). In typical Gothic novel fashion, Jane finds herself in the labyrinth of Thornfield Hall threatened by the aristocratic and Byronic Edward Fairfax Rochester. Jane, like Isabella, Emily, and Antonia, is highly perceptive and a skillful investigator; indeed, like the Gothic heroines who precede her, her perceptual acumen results in a troubled reality principle where quasi-supernatural occurrences happen, although they are often by materialistic explanations. Although we might take issue with Jane Eyre's plot resolution in her salvation-by-marriage with Rochester, when compared to the fate of previous Gothic heroines, we can see how her perceptual acuity has become a source of power and agency in this novel.

THE GOTHIC HEROINE IN THE MODERN ERA

As we take a wide-angled perspective on the evolution of the Gothic heroine, surprising features begin to reveal themselves as writers and filmmakers reproduce her in changing modern contexts. The Gothic heroine continues to be marked, first and foremost, by her radical sensitivity and perceptual acuity, her powerful, nearly omniscient sensorium, although the extent to which this perceptual acuity lends her agency or results in her victimization is ambiguous throughout several texts. For example, consider Henry James' Governess at Bly, the protagonist of his novella *The Turn of the Screw* (1898). Like Jane Eyre, Antonia, Emily St. Aubert, and Isabella, the Governess of Bly finds herself in a haunted labyrinth and, due to her perceptual acuity, is able to see through the reality principle, the patriarchically-inflected ordinary/order; however, her visions of the supernatural do not result in agency, as in the case of Jane Eyre, but in emotional instability. The novel famously ends in mystery. We never know if the governess is a successful exorcist or a paranoid who has accidently murdered a child.

In her mental instability, the Governess at Bly alludes to another famous Gothic heroine, the protagonist of Charlotte Gilman Perkin's transparently feminist/activist "The Yellow Wallpaper" (1892). Like the Gothic heroines who precede her, this young woman is characteristically sensitive and compelled to scrutinize her small world, a room plastered with yellow wallpaper; however, her excessive scrutiny and perceptual power results in her descent into madness when she recognizes a pattern in the hideous wallpaper of her room, something like an occult message that reveals the nature of her subjection to arbitrary patriarchal authority in the form of male-dominated psychiatry.

The Gothic heroine's compelling imbrication with psychic power and psychological pathology evolves throughout the twentieth century. Indeed, the Gothic heroine becomes not only merely a madwomen in the attic but a demon-possessed alien goddesses, psycho-kinetic madwomen, whose excess power needs to be domesticated and regulated by male pedagogical treatment. Let me briefly survey this development.

PSYCHO-KINETIC MADWOMEN

One interesting modern Gothic heroine that demonstrates this evolution is the paranormally sensitive Eleanor Vance of Shirley Jackson's *The Haunting of Hill House* (1959). Eleanor Vance is an echo of the Gothic heroine of "The

Yellow Wallpaper" to the extent that she, too, descends into madness at the end of the novel due to perceptual acuity, psychic power, and psychological pathology. Her fusion with the haunted house and supernatural agency that occupies it anticipates later incarnations of the Gothic heroine/antagonist as monster/victim, such as William Peter Blatty's Regan Blair in *The Exorcist* (1973).

The Exorcist, adapted from William Peter Blatty's 1971 novel of the same name, narrates the demonic possession of another Gothic heroine, the 12-year-old Regan MacNeil. Not only does Regan demonstrate defiance in the face of patriarchal power figures, such as a series of doctors, engineers, and priests, she is also radically transgressive regarding sexual and religious taboos. I will not rehearse the many ways Regan trangresses against an the "male ordinary" in the story, such as, for example, masturbating with a crucifix, but I see her demonic possession as a male fictionalization of transgression associated with the actual transgression of the Women's Liberation movement concurrent with the film's release. From this perspective, the exorcism of Regan becomes less a form of spiritual liberation and more a form of patriarchal domestication of radically transgressive femininity at odds with the patriarchal order.

Blatty's Regan MacNeil is not the only demon-haunted, Gothic heroine fictionalized to reconcile and resolve the inherent contradictions of patriarchal society. Carrie White, the Gothic heroine of Stephen King's novel, *Carrie*, adapted into a memorable horror film released in 1976, symptomatizes and responds to similar tensions as well, and in similar symbolic ways. Like Regan, Carrie White manifests great power that is constrained and feared by a patriarchy transferred in this film onto to other male-abused women—e.g., Carrie's religiously fanatical mother, Margaret, and the high school bully, Chris Hergesen. King admits that his novel is a feminist allegory in his popular critical account of horror titled, *Danse Macabre* (1951). Of *Carrie*, he writes, "*Carrie* is largely about how women find their own channels of power, and what men fear about women's sexuality . . . writing the book in 1973 . . . I was fully aware of what Woman's Liberation implied. The book is . . . an uneasy masculine shrinking from a future of female equality."[6] This compelling insight into the masculinist fears that inspired the novel and film needs to be paired, however, with other comments King made, such as in an April 1981 interview published in the first issue of a short-lived *Twilight Zone Magazine*. Discussing the genesis of the story, King states, "Some woman said, 'You write all those macho things, but you can't write about women.' I said, 'I'm not scared of women. I could write about them if I wanted to.' So I got an idea for a story about this incident in a girl's shower room and the girl would be telekinetic. The other girls would pelt her with sanitary napkins when she got her period. The period would release the right hormones and she would rain down destruction on them."[7]

Juxtaposing this comment against King's own politically-charged allegorical reading of *Carrie* allows us to view Carrie White not only as a rendering of a dangerously powerful menstruating and liberated woman but also as a male-regulated secret agent of an absent male controller/author. From King's perspective, Carrie White belongs to him; she is his, his clever artistic creation, his powerful, menstruating woman, capable not only of using her mind to kill but, more importantly, of contradicting any other woman who would dare to challenge his lack of female insight. King, working in the genre of modern Gothic, a genre formally unconstrained by a reality principle, responds to female critics by giving full vent to the inescapable forces of distortion that haunt any and all attempts to represent women as radically "Other," as fundamentally different and non-male. Why? Because women, as humans, are not so very different from men, and men, as humans, are not so very different from women, a dangerous doctrine supremely toxic to the maintenance and policing of the patriarchal ideological order that depends upon difference.

The idea that women are not human, are irredeemably Other, conditions many male renderings of the Gothic heroine as a psycho-kinetic madwoman in the literature and popular culture of the 1980s and 1990s, and acutely so in the case of science fiction. Several examples abound: the xenomorphically-sensitive Ripley in Ridley Scott's *Alien*, the digital temptress of John Hughes' *Weird Science*, the deadly Sil of Roger Donaldson's *Species*, the Borg-queen of *Star Trek: First Contact*. As male-renderings of psychologically tortured Gothic heroines proceed in lock step to changes in Western conceptions of woman, perhaps an encouraging ambivalence enters. What is this ambivalence? The Gothic heroine is often, though not always, fictionalized as good, when properly domesticated and controlled by a regulating male pedagogue or controller, of course, such as in Luc Besson's *The Fifth Element*, a film that narrates the relationship between a male police officer and a goddess alien named Leloo. Leloo, for all intents and purposes, is a Gothic heroine whose power is cosmic in scope; she is able not only to defeat men in martial arts battles but also to save entire planets from errant, moon-sized meteors. But, despite her unfathomable reservoirs of power, she needs the romantic sanctioning of the patriarchal order to liberate her from debilitating depression. Despite her awesome power, her stature as a planet-saving goddess, Leloo nevertheless requires the sanctioning in the form of a kiss from Corbin Dallas, a police officer, who regularly and anxiously reports to a room of anxious, impatient men—generals and the president—about its progress.

Leloo Dallas is not the only male-rendered, demon-haunted, powerful, and Gothic heroine who needs protection and regulation by men in popular science fiction film and television. She brings to mind the mysterious River Tam, a mentally ill, psycho-kinetically powerful prophetess who requires the constant surveillance and attention of her caring brother, a doctor, Simon Tam, who always has his tranquilizers near at hand. Like Regan, Carrie, Leloo, and many others, the unreal, male-rendered Gothic heroine River Tam possesses limitless power but is always on the verge mental collapse, and would collapse if not for the support of her loving, and regulating, brother.

With Regan, Carrie, Leloo, and River Tam, we can see a sinister pattern emerging: in popular medias unconstrained by the reality principle, male writers are able to allow the logic of their ideologically-functional fantasies of sexually alluring and powerful Gothic heroines to bloom into their full dark glory. In these works, we can catch glimpses of what cultural critic Frederic calls "the political unconscious": these powerful renderings are epideictic gestures for resolving contradictions, for maintaining a toxic gender difference that doesn't, in reality, exist at all, i.e., for hiding the reality that womanhood is a subjectivity projected by a sexless tribe onto a sexless tribe to maintain arbitrary power.[8]

Let me conclude this brief survey of the modern Gothic heroine with one final psycho-kinetic madwoman from a more recent incarnation of the Gothic, a character who, from my perspective, reveals an encouraging limit approaching: "Eleven," the Gothic heroine of the Duffer Brother's *Stranger Things* (2016).

Like Regan, Eleven is demon-haunted, and like Carrie, she is gifted with psycho-kinetic powers. Desperate for human connection and pedagogical guidance, like Leloo, she is also regulated by the medical gaze of her Papa, Dr. Brenner, and the harsh policing of her erstwhile guardian, Jim Hopper. In one of the final episodes, gazing into a forest pool, Eleven has an epiphany, removes her wig, and goes and saves her friends form bullies, and almost kills in doing so. Her friends, appalled by her violent display, berate her. Here is where the character tests the ideological limits of the narrative. Object of their adolescent, male-fantasy gaze, she says this: "I'm the monster."

From the perspective of ideological critique, thus modern Gothic heroine is saying something truthful: subjected to the regulation of men who fear her, initiated into the mystery that she bears of the wound of radical difference, she does represent great power. Without her wig, she looks not very different from the boys looking upon her and the boys look not very different from. Sexless, she denies her radical difference. To the extent that she troubles gender ideology, Eleven's radical strangeness tears of the very fabric of reality, i.e., the ordinary that supports patriarchy, white supremacy, and capitalism, and the violence these systems fuel.

CONCLUSION: GOTHIC HEROINE TO "GOTH" GIRL

In the case of the haunted and psycho-kinetically powerful Eleanor Vance, Regan Blair, Carrie White, and Eleven, the Gothic protagonist manifests psychic powers that are a logical outgrowth and formal reproduction of her initial perceptual/mental acuity that surfaces as early as Isabella in *The Castle of Otranto*. The seed of the Gothic heroine's psychic power is there from the beginning of the Gothic novel waiting to bloom.

Let me conclude with a surprising iteration of the Gothic heroine whose perceptual acuity manifests in a virtual world where, arguably, the reality principle is not violated at all. Consider Allison Reynolds (Ally Sheedy), a Goth girl from John Hughes' *The Breakfast Club* (1985). Like the Gothic heroines before her, Allison's distinctiveness derives from her quasi-omniscience, her powerful sensorium, an inheritance of the eighteenth-, nineteenth-, and twentieth-century terrorized Gothic heroines who preceded her. Let me conclude with a brief scene from Hughes' original screenplay: the teenage Brian Johnson (Anthony Michael Hall) and Andrew Clark (Emilio Estevez) are passing time in detention and a darkly clad Allison hanging back, watching these young men socialize. Andrew asks Brian, "You got a middle name?" Before Brian can answer, Allison, unprompted, interrupts their conversation:

"Your middle name is Ralph, as in puke. Your birthday is March 12th, you're five-nine and a half you weigh a hundred and thirty pounds and your social security number is 0-4-9-3-8-0-9-1 (a beat) 3."

Andrew, impressed, responds, "Wow! Are you psychic?"

The Gothic heroine is a trope that artists in the Gothic tradition continue to reproduce. She is defined by her powerful sensorium, her acute sensitivity, and this psychic power often manifests as either monstrosity, or, as in the case of John Hughes' Allison Reynold's in *The Breakfast Club*, an acute awareness of the threatening nature of a dangerous world structured by patriarchy.

NOTES

1. Georg Lukács, "Reification and the Consciousness of the Proletariat," in *History and Class Consciousness*, trans. Rodney Livingstone (Cambridge: MIT Press, 1971), 83–222. "Reification" refers to the process of making something abstract, dependent, and unreal into something concrete, autonomous, and real; it is has been incorporated by literary scholars by way of Marxist theory, particular via the work of Georg Lukács, in whose essay "Reification and the Consciousness of the Proletariat" (1923) the term rises to prominence.

2. Fred Botting, *Gothic* (London: Routledge, 1995).

3. Christopher Pittard, "The Victorian Context: Serialization, Circulation, Genres," in *Bloomsbury Introduction to Popular Literature*, ed. Christine Berberich (London: Bloomsbury, 2014), 11–29. Pittard provides a succinct historical survey of Anglophone (mostly British) popular fiction readers and their reading habits prior to the twentieth century.

4. Ian Watt, *The Rise of the Novel* (Oakland: University of California Press, 2001). Watt's classic account of the novel continues to be the authoritative history of literary realism.

5. Noel Carroll, *The Philosophy of Horror* (London: Routledge, 1990). Carroll provides a nuanced account the related aesthetic categories of "horror," "terror," and "fear."

6. Stephen King, *Dans Macabre* (New York: Berkley, 1981), 171.

7. Stephen King, "I Like to Go for the Jugular," in *Twilight Zone Magazine* 1, no. 1 (April 1981), 108.

8. Fredric Jameson, *The Political Unconscious: Narrative as a Socially Symbolic Act* (New York: Cornell University Press, 1981).

REFERENCES

Botting, Fred. *Gothic.* London: Routledge, 1995.

Carroll, Noel. *The Philosophy of Horror.* London: Routledge, 1990.

Jameson, Fredric. *The Political Unconscious: Narrative as a Socially Symbolic Act.* New York: Cornell University Press, 1981.

King, Stephen. *Dans Macabre.* New York: Berkley, 1981.

King, Stephen. "I Like to Go for the Jugular," in *Twilight Zone Magazine* 1, no. 1. April 1981.

Lukács, Georg. "Reification and the Consciousness of the Proletariat," in *History and Class Consciousness*, trans. Rodney Livingstone. Cambridge: MIT Press, 1971.

Pittard, Christopher. "The Victorian Context: Serialization, Circulation, Genres," in *Bloomsbury Introduction to Popular Literature*, ed. Christine Berberich. London: Bloomsbury, 2014.

Watt, Ian. *The Rise of the Novel.* Oakland: University of California Press, 2001.

Chapter Four

Democracy and the Limitations on Women's Rights

Ursula Scheidegger

I am interested in the structural, social, and cultural aspects that limit the involvement and the influence of women in democratic politics, despite equality and the right to political participation. My deeper engagement with this topic started in the context of a project: Safeguarding Democracy: Contests of Values and Interests, which was an academic partnership between a South African and a Swiss university. In this project, we moved away from an approach relatively common in such collaboration that is looking at the democratic deficits in the global south in relations to so called stable and consolidated democracies in the north. Typically, when we engage with democracy, we tend to have specific assumptions and expectations about different countries that influence the questions we ask in order to assess democratic institutions and performance. Instead in this project, we examined how democracies differ in the ways they put democratic ideals into practice and organize political participation and representation. This not only included the historical context and narratives of the origin of democracy but also involved values and beliefs, attitudes, social hierarchies and power that shaped the democratization process from early attempts to create democratic structures to the building of institutions and the setting of rules that govern democratic practice.

After having lived and worked for more than 20 years in South Africa, it was interesting for me to have a look at Switzerland, my home country, that prides itself to be one of the oldest democracies, although women got the right to vote only in 1971. The fact that Switzerland is widely regarded as one of the most stable and established democracies proves how assumptions about a country not only influence assessments of its history and politics but also tend to prevent a meaningful engagement with the problematic sides of its political and democratic development. In addition, the Swiss system of direct democracy is considered to be more democratic as it extends the right to vote beyond elections to plebiscites ranging from voting on the introduction of new legislation to changes of existing legislation or the allocation of resources. Also in this context, there is little examination of the negative aspects of plebiscites, not only in terms of issues put to the vote, but also in terms of the inequalities with respect to power and resources that dominate voting campaigns, exclusions from the right to vote and the effects, that outcomes of plebiscites may have on individuals and groups. An appropriate example is the plebiscite to introduce the women's vote in Switzerland that was rejected by Swiss men in 1959.

The engagement with the Swiss system and its history of democracy offers a good case study to examine the limitations of democracies and the impact this has on people's lives and opportunities. Despite the distinctive history and development of democracy in Switzerland and the system of direct democracy, the Swiss example is not unique. The conflicts between democratic values and particular interest in a context of unequal access to power and resources are inherent to struggles for emancipation. Moreover, the example of Swiss women not only demonstrates the consequences political exclusion and the limitations of rights have on the lives of human beings, but also the time and processes that were and still are necessary to amend the damages done to individuals and groups by injustice and a system of discrimination. The Swiss example also shows that equal rights and political participation are not sufficient because the social, economic, and institutional context offers or limits spaces of personal development and engagement. We have to differentiate between legal rights and substantives rights, in other words we have to look at the spaces in which women can exercise their rights effectively and at the opportunities, they enjoy. Finally, because democracies have limitations and democratic systems are vulnerable due to the unequal access to power and resources, it is necessary to have a set of overarching rights and values that are not negotiable, for example human rights, dignity, and personal freedom in order to safeguard democracy from powerful interests and the destructive potential of the electorate.

Two core features of democracies are representation and the vote. Representation is based on the ideal that citizens from all segments of society send representatives to parliament and hence have a voice promoting their demands and concerns and communicating their grievances. In practice, election campaigns and the result of elections demonstrate that only resourceful and well connected citizens with a public profile have a chance to be elected and parliament represents rather different interests groups than the diversity of the entire population. This is reflected in the composition of parliament in terms of gender, origin, color of skin, and socioeconomic stratum, religion, education, profession, age, language, and region. Nevertheless, representation is critical in terms of which demands and concerns are considered important to be included in debates, the setting of the political agenda and the allocation of resources. Women still do most of the unpaid care work, have less access to the labor market, are discriminated by the pay gap and poverty is more prevalent among women and children. Due to the prevailing organization of family life in Switzerland, especially after the arrival of children, many women subordinate their professional engagement to their family obligations. In contrast, for men professional activities have priority over family commitments. The institutional and social context from school time tables to public services and opening hours of clinics or shops and the limited availability of childcare facilities reflect assumptions about the role and availability of mothers. Consequently, the social, institutional, and political context contribute to the perpetuation of unequal opportunities for women.[1] Political engagement of women is similar to their professional development a problem in the context of family duties, even more so on the national level, as parliament and parliamentary commissions convene in the capital, Bern, and not in the region where women live. In addition to the difficulty of coordinating professional and family responsibilities, stereotypes and prejudices about women's role in society intersect with origin, socioeconomic class, religion, age, education, or color of skin. This not only enables or reduces opportunities of political engagement but also influences the public profile of women and impacts on women's space of political activity and their chances of getting elected.

The late introduction of the women's vote in Switzerland offers insights into the difficulties women experienced after attaining the right for political participation. The vote for women was introduced in February 1971, for the national elections in October of the same year, the lacking public profile of female politicians was a challenge. Not only levels of education, origin, and socioeconomic class but also region in the federal system of Switzerland, where cantons (provinces) enjoy a considerable degree of autonomy, impacted on the election campaigns of individual women. After the failure to introduce political rights for women in 1959, the struggle for the women's vote intensified in the 1960s. Increasingly well educated women were in a professional position that were incompatible with their lacking political and social rights. A new generation of women confronted traditional gender roles, which included educational and professional opportunities, access to the workplace, the pay gap, the contestation of traditional family structures and access to family planning and abortion. Political manifestations became more frequent and more confrontational, sometimes at a considerable personal risk, for example the demand of access to safe abortions in Catholic cantons. The connections to women's movement in other countries broadened the interactions of civil society organizations and the increasing numbers of television sets in Swiss households brought social struggles to the living rooms of Swiss families. A growing number of social movements, not only women's organization started to challenge traditional politics and values from the military (Switzerland has a draft) to environmental concerns, the power of the corporate sector, LGTB, the welfare state to social problems such as violence and poverty. In addition, a number of cantons introduced the vote for women on the cantonal level. The Canton of Vaud and the Canton of Neuchatel already introduced the vote for women in 1959, the same year it was rejected on the national level.

Only 11 women were elected in 1971, the first parliamentary elections in which they were allowed to participate (10 to the 200 seat national council, 1 to the then 44 seat council of states). In the nearly 50 years that have passed since then, the situation has improved, but the number of women in parliament has not reached a critical mass, after the last national elections in 2015, only 32 percent of the national council and 15.2 percent of the council of states were women.[2] Equally underrepresented are women in institutions such as courts, office of the prosecutor and in federal ministries and directorates. Moreover, women didn't have the right to vote in local elections and plebiscite in a number of cantons despite the introduction of the right to vote on the national level.

Beside the unequal distribution of opportunities and burdens, for a long time, Swiss men considered it normal that women have no voice. The exclusion of women from politics, their lacking representation and perceptions of traditional gender roles had and still have an impact on assumptions about the competence and abilities of women in public office. The formation and consolidation of social values regarding the status of women in society is historically constructed and tends to outlive political, economic, and social transformation. As women for a long time were legally excluded from the vote, the stigma that they are unfit to participate is perpetuated as their underrepresentation enforces perceptions that women are not as able as men to serve in political office.[3] In addition, stereotypical ideas about women's abilities to perform in leadership positions are influenced by gender specific socialization. Values that originate in tradition, history, and heritage together with levels of social control by dominant groups inform the political culture and influence political behavior.[4] In other words, there is a correlation between particular histories, the dominant culture and political and social practice. Or, as Nancy Fraser argues, the effects of exclusion are not amended by the acknowledgment and implementation of rights because of the underlying value structure.[5] Today, the resurgence of nationalist politics and the invocation of to the "good old days" by conservative and right wing parties increases the challenges for women, as they refer to a time where the place of women was in the family and not in the public sphere. This is, for example, reflected in the shift of what is acceptable or tolerated in verbal attacks against women who challenge traditional norms and gender roles.

Mary Beard argues in her book *Women and Power* that the quest for representation and political power by women was for centuries, and still continues to be, a difficult mission. Professional achievements, competence and leadership qualities of women are not only scrutinized, their integrity is also criticized and undermined, often in quite emotional attacks, displaying a worrying level of misogyny and demonstrating where the place of women is in society.[6] Melissa Harris-Perry in her book *Sister Citizen* introduces the concepts hateful stereotypes and the crooked room to refer to a context where women experience predisposition, bias, and prejudice instead of impartiality, objectivity, and fairness in political, social, and professional contexts. Hateful stereotypes undermine women's competence, abilities, and accomplishments and intersect with race, class, or origin. They not only limit or potentially destroy opportunities and career options but also impact on confidence, self-esteem, recognition, and dignity.[7] Hateful stereotypes cause distortions, pain, and injustice. In Switzerland, stereotypes also impact the social mobility of women. Despite efforts to move away from gender-specific career choices, there are still professions with a much higher proportion of women. Due to the stratification in the labor market, the persistence of gender specific sectors contribute to the pay gap and the lower position of women in professional hierarchies.[8] To sum it up, women face more obstacles and need higher professional qualification in order to promote their careers and increase their chances to attain a higher professional position, get elected into parliament, and enjoy the recognition they deserve.

Newcomers face challenges in established political structures. There tends to be a certain mistrust and reservations toward newcomers. Dominant groups like to see themselves better as less experienced politicians or minorities and they try to gain political capital at the expense of newcomers who may question or challenge the political agenda and present new ideas. Strategies to disempower and undermine unwanted contenders range from attacking their integrity and competence, exploiting hateful stereotypes, pointing at the role and place of women in society to debasement, ridicule, and mockery. In addition, it is difficult to gain access to lobby groups. In contrast to official interests or lobby groups, where membership has to be disclosed, there are informal networks based on personal relations. They operate behind closed doors, providing considerable levels of social and political capital and influence politics as gatekeepers, by manipulating political processes, promoting and supporting protégés and friends and by the selective dissemination of information or the circulation of rumors and fake news. The nature of these networks makes it difficult to assess their significance, weight, impact, and consequences. In Switzerland, it is in the labor market and the military (Switzerland has a draft) where personal relations are forged. In both structures women are either underrepresented or have limited access.

Switzerland is also an example of how exclusion and lacking political representation has affected the lives of women and their rights and opportunities. Women depended on men in all important aspects of their existence from their status in society, their dignity and the respect, they enjoy to professional development opportunities, the family, the rights over their bodies to social welfare and the protection from violence. We shouldn't forget that the status of women in society as well as the respect and recognition they enjoy have a critical impact on women's dignity and the levels of violence against them. In addition, lacking representation limited the options of advocacy in favor of women in order to address their demands and grievances. In Switzerland, dominant perceptions of gender roles promoted men's career over that of women, salaries of women were lower than that of men in comparable positions, men were the sole heads of the family, divorce law privileged men, not to mention the treatment of poor women or single mothers, who were considered indolent, irresponsible, and morally inferior. Legislation allowed for draconian punishment of deviant women and at the same time, a culture of lenience, trivialization, and a sense of impunity offered men spaces to avoid responsibility and escape the consequences of problematic behavior, such as the use of violence and physical and psychological abuse. It is interesting to look at the campaign in the run-up for the plebiscite to introduce the right of women to vote in 1959, in which Swiss only men were allowed to vote. It was argued that the majority of women didn't want the vote; that the home was the place for women, that the nature of women was incompatible with politics, that women involved in politics might lose their femininity; that politics were too dirty and insecure for women; that politics could corrupt women; and last, but not least, that women interested in politics could voice their opinion and demands via their spouses.[9] In other words, the lacking representation of women in parliament enabled men to ignore areas vital to women's lives and promote an agenda they considered appropriate for women. It was based on the perception of women as mothers and wives in the nuclear family. As a result, women pursuing a professional career, independent, unmarried women, lesbians or single mothers did not fit into the gender roles assigned to them and were considered to be a problem. It was in a social context that not only limited the autonomy and opportunities of women, it also suited Swiss men, as the exclusion from political participation made it more challenging for women to change their position. Moreover, there was little incentive for male politicians to change a situation that benefitted them.

Only in 1974 for the first time, a report on the position and well-being of women in family and society was published.[10] However, it was commissioned by UNESCO and not the Swiss government. The report started with a critical discussion of dominant norms and values regarding the role of women in society; norms and values that not only justified differences in socialization and education but also prevented any significant engagement with the limitations on opportunities and choices and levels of discrimination.[11] Different standards of education prepared men and women for their different roles and place in society, further limiting education of women in an educational system that was already inferior in comparison to other highly developed countries.[12] Discrimination of women in the labor market was (and still is) reflected in lower salaries and constraints on career opportunities. Arguments justifying inequalities ranged from pregnancy to women being more emotional, less capable to deal with stress to lacking leadership qualities.[13] Moreover, at the time of the report, there was little reflection on the power distribution in the family, women were in charge of care provisions toward husband and children, adopted their husbands name and place of origin or nationality. Men were financially responsible, represented the family and had decision-making power in all important areas of family life.[14] Women and mothers who didn't fit into this model were stigmatized. Unmarried mothers or mothers who continued to work and pursue a professional career outside the family or had to work out of financial necessity had not only to cope with high stress levels by the double burden of family and work but also were considered to undermine the healthy development of their children.[15]

The report also provided data on the well-being of women, levels of stress due to high demands and expectations, the problem of isolation and loneliness in nuclear families, and the stage in life when children have left home. The report provoked different reactions from disbelief, denial, refusal, and critique to support, endorsement, and approval. Among women, the awareness or denial of one's personal situation and perceptions of injustice and discrimination depended on a number of factors from education, self-consciousness, location such as urban versus rural, progressive versus conservative cantons or socioeconomic stratum. There was also acceptance and approval of male dominance among women due to lacking self-worth and feelings of inferiority.[16] Nevertheless, the report offered opportunities as for the first time, reliable data was available on the position of women in family and society, their dependencies, perceptions of well-being, constraints on their choices and opportunities and for a long time the lacking agency to change their situation due to the absence of political rights.

Beside the problems emanating from structural violence, another area of neglect and ignorance was physical violence and abuse against women. In the 1970s, different women's organizations started to collect data and establish shelters for survivors of violence in bigger cities. In a number of cantons the local governments initiated first surveys on the extent and frequency of violence against women by approaching doctors, clerics, social workers, and the police. In March 1980, a female member of the national parliament requested a first national report on violence and abuse against women.[17] The report was published in 1982 and provided a first overview of the extent of violence and abuse.[18] It started the long overdue debate on the problem. The report elicited different reactions, from disbelief and denial to the recognition that violence against women is a problem that needs to be addressed. The report provided data in order to develop and implement legislation for the protection of women. It was a conflictual process, due to controversial views about women and their rights, place and role in society and disagreement about the boundaries between the private and the public spheres, especially in the context of legal interventions in cases of domestic violence. In addition, the acknowledgment that the prevention of violence against women is a collective problem was contested and the correlation between the respect women enjoy and their rights and status in society and levels of violence disputed. Both reports are compelling examples of the consequences caused by the marginalization and discrimination of women on their well-being, their opportunities but also in terms of their protection and safety. As long as women didn't have the vote, they would not become a threat to the election of aspiring politicians nor would they have any impact on resource allocation or priorities on the political agenda.

The right to vote is another important feature of democracies, however, as the struggle of Swiss women shows, there is the problem of who has the right to vote. In addition, voting systems are susceptible to manipulation not only on the organizational and structural level but also especially during election campaigns. Democracies are dynamic systems and have to be constantly negotiated in order to accommodate new developments; for example, the availability of modern technology and response to changing expectations of the population based on principles and rights that limit the power of well established citizens or corporate entities in order to guarantee equality and justice. Instead of respect, fairness, rationality, honesty, and impartiality, election systems are marked by vast differences in resources and political and social capital. Campaigns become increasingly exclusive, divisive, and emotionally driven. The emphasis of election outcomes that conflate the majority, sometimes by a small margin, with the will of the people are potentially discriminating and limit rights, opportunities and choices of minorities or human beings that do not fit into the dominant perceptions of social roles. Hence, democratic systems are vulnerable as the unequal access to power and resources is not effectively addressed and restrained in order to level the playing field in the political arena. The German sociologist Claus Offe warns that democracies face the danger of self-destruction through electoral majoritarian rule.[19] Even though we consider the vote as one of the most democratic expression of political participation, the question arises whether it was really democratic that in one of the "oldest democracies of the world" only Swiss men were allowed to decide on the right of women to vote in a referendum. Swiss men rejected the vote for women on February 1, 1959, with 66.9 percent no votes versus 33.1 percent yes votes.[20] Finally, Swiss men agreed to the vote for women on February 7, 1971, this time with 65.7 percent yes votes versus 34.3 percent no votes.[21] Nevertheless, the introduction of the women's vote in Switzerland did not change automatically all legal discrimination of women. The struggle continued; for example, with respect to equality of women and men in the Swiss constitution or the amendments of marriage and divorce law and the protection of women from all forms of violence and abuse. Since representation of women in parliament was so low, civil society continued to be an important driver of women's rights and demands. Equality for women and men in the Swiss constitution was only introduced in 1981, after a plebiscite with an approval rate of 60 percent.[22] The new marriage law was introduced in 1985, again after a plebiscite and with a nearly 55 percent approval rate only.[23] Legislation to make violence in marriage and partnership an official offense was launched in 1996 and only introduced by the Swiss parliament in 2003.[24]

The Swiss example demonstrates how critical it is that democracies are also based on overarching values and rights that are fundamental and defining institutions such as human rights, dignity, and personal freedoms. The shortcomings of democracies inherent in the right to vote and representation have to be balanced with a set of rights and values that guarantee justice, protect the rights of everyone, and limit the destructive potential of the electorate. Democracy is a space of choices and opportunities to pursue one's aspiration to lead a fulfilled life and that includes less powerful and resourceful citizens in a context of mutual respect, rights, and obligations. Moreover, spaces of choice not only have to accommodate different views of society and gender roles, but also require the necessary tolerance to allow for legal and regulatory provision that don't limit agency and choices of those with different opinions, worldviews, and norms. This must be in a context that is regulated and limited by the constitution, and in a legal system that is fair and impartial. These rights are the foundations of democracies, and hence are beyond the deliberations and negotiations of daily politics or electoral contestation. Human rights should at least protect and enable human beings to live in an environment with the necessary provisions of food, shelter, access to education and healthcare, the freedom to make choices on important matters in their lives and to be safe from discrimination, exclusion, and the limitation of oppressive political or traditional systems. Collective and cultural rights have to be negotiated in a way that individuals have a choice to take part in tradition, religion, or cultural institutions and not in a way that cultural, collective, or traditional groups have a claim on individuals. This is especially important in the context of women's rights.

Switzerland is proud of its cultural and linguistic diversity but it also has to face the challenges of accommodating different language groups, minorities, religions, or cultural groups. Hence, tolerance, respect for others, con-sociationalism, and the political will to compromise are at least promoted as critical aspects of the political culture. Nevertheless, women's rights were for a long time a blind spot. Debates on human rights are a more recent development. Often human rights are perceived as not relevant for Switzerland but rather needed in non-democratic countries with high levels of violence, corruption, discrimination, and a biased legal system. There is also little awareness of reports, international conventions and treaties, women's organizations are more influenced by the international women's movement than by human rights. More engagement would enable legislators to address shortfalls in areas such as equal pay, sexual discrimination, reproductive rights, welfare, migration, and racial profiling. On the other hand, nationalist movements and parties increasingly attack human rights, politicizing and undermining them as they consider human rights in conflict with Swiss rights and tradition and not in the interest of the population. The Swiss People's Party even has launched a plebiscite against the primacy of international legislation based on the Universal Declaration of Human Rights and the European Convention of Human Rights: Self-Determination, Swiss Law instead of Foreign Judges. Fortunately, it was rejected in the plebiscite on November 25, 2018 by 66.2 percent of the voters.[25] Nevertheless, disagreement and dispute around human rights continue, one of the more recent developments, not only in Switzerland, is to limit or deny human rights in the context of migration or terrorism prevention. The threat to human rights has increased debates on human rights and the acknowledgment of the importance of an independent watchdog in order to address the shortcomings of democratic systems in terms of representation, conflicts between rights and power and values and interests.

There is a further context in which Switzerland demonstrates the importance of overarching values, such as human rights, freedom, and equality. Switzerland couldn't ignore the beginnings of the European Union (EU) as trade, commerce, financial institutions, and services depended on the cooperation with the EU. Switzerland became an active member of the European Council in 1963. After the horrors of World War II and the Universal Declaration of Human Rights, the nascent European Community focused on conflict elimination and peace building along with the establishment of economic cooperation. In this context of peace promotion, the European Convention of Human Rights (ECHR) was launched as the underlying ethical framework guiding EU politics. It was signed and implemented by the then member states of the European Community in 1950. Over time, the adoption of the ECHR became one of the conditions in order to join the European Council or negotiate economic relations as a non-member of the EU. In 1963, one of the "oldest democracies" in the world couldn't sign the ECHR because of lacking the vote for women. As a consequence, Swiss women had additional leverage in their struggle for the vote in the run-up to the 1971 plebiscite on the introduction of women's political rights. As already mentioned, finally, in 1971, a majority of Swiss men voted in favor of the vote for women. However, in the context of the emerging European Community, it is not clear whether this decision was based on democratic values or economic interests. In case of the latter, unfortunately stereotypes and prejudices against women in politics are perpetuated. Moreover, there was and still is little engagement with the consequences of lacking rights and the injustice women experienced due to their discrimination. For example a Swiss historian considered the introduction of the women's vote a minor modification of the Swiss democratic system.[26] Political rights and the vote for women were a critical and overdue adjustment paving the way for the introduction and implementation of equal rights and personal freedoms for women and finally starting to eliminate discrimination and injustice. The fact that the vote of Swiss men as a democratic instrument had more weight than the rights of women is an example of the vulnerability and limitation of democratic systems. Nevertheless, as already mentioned, despite the introduction of the vote for women on the national level in 1971, a number of cantons introduced the vote for women later. In the last canton, Appenzell Innerrhoden, men denied women the right to vote on the cantonal level again in a plebiscite in April 1990. As equality between women and men was introduced in the Swiss constitution in 1981, women were constitutionally entitled to political rights and the outcome of the plebiscite was overruled by the Federal Supreme Court of Switzerland.

Nearly 50 years after the introduction of the women's vote in Switzerland and the amendments of the constitution and laws providing for equal rights, there are still unfair differences in terms of political representation of women, equal pay, career opportunities, the burden of care provisions, levels of poverty, and incidences of violence. There are a number of achievements, but they are under threat by conservative politics and the traditional gender roles they promote. Assertions that women have equal right and that it is up to women to claim them disregard the complexity of the political, social, and economic context and the contestations between values and interests. Equal rights do not translate into equal opportunities and do not eliminate all areas of discrimination. René Levy, co-author of the study *The Position of Women in Family and Society* has investigated the choices of young couples especially when they become parents. He argues that due to the lack of child care provisions, young parents fall back into traditional gender roles against their ideals. Plans to promote the professional careers of both parents and share the care burden fail not because of the lacking will of young parents but because they have no other option. In addition, due to the federal system, there are considerable differences in terms of child care provisions and cost in different cantons. In the current situation, well resourced parents have more opportunities to find alternatives to missing state provisions for childcare; nevertheless, this increases social inequality. State institutions can promote, influence, and encourage social change. For example, the provision of child care facilities would not only be one of the critical measures toward more equality of women and men but also contribute to a change in the perceptions of women's role in society. Levy argues that it is easier to address institutional deficiencies than the mentality of citizens; moreover, institutional changes contribute to the transformation of social attitudes.[27] It seems like a vicious circle: on the one hand, women's representation is still below the critical mass in order to promote their demands for child care; on the other hand, the problem of child care makes it more challenging for women to get involved in politics.

In conclusion, the struggle for women's rights in Switzerland is a good example of the limitations and challenges of democracy. It demonstrates the importance of human rights and personal freedoms as a fundamental aspect of the democratic state. Despite its particular history, the Swiss example reveals broader shortcomings and vulnerabilities of democratic systems including in "older," more consolidated democracies. Switzerland also shows how expectations and assumptions about different countries influence the ways we assess democratic institutions and outcomes. Moreover, it is a good example of how widespread narratives about the past are in conflict with historical development and realities.

Democratic systems are susceptible to manipulation. There are limited options to intervene in order to balance the unequal access to power and resources. On the contrary, due to the leverage of powerful and well-resourced politicians there is little political will to address the deficiencies that benefit them. Contests between values and specific interests occur in a context where access to power and resources is unequally distributed and where powerful interests potentially undermine democratic values.

Representation is one of the core aspects of democracy; however, the diversity of society is not reflected in the composition of parliament. Women face a number of challenges entering the political arena and building the necessary public profile. Tradition, history, and heritage inform the political culture and influence political behavior and they outlive political and social transformation. The persistent underrepresentation of women enforces stereotypes about the capabilities of women in politics. Competence, professional achievements, and leadership qualities of women are scrutinized. At the same time, bias, prejudice, and hateful stereotypes display a worrying level of misogyny and undermine opportunities and careers. The resurgence of nationalist politics and the invocation of the "good old days" by conservative and right wing parties refer to a time where the place of women was in the family. Furthermore, women still do most of the unpaid care work, have less access to the labor market, are discriminated by the pay gap and poverty is more prevalent among women and children. Due to the prevailing organization of family life in Switzerland, especially after the arrival of children, women tend to subordinate their professional or political engagement to their family obligations. This is enforced by an institutional and social context that counts on the availability of women from school time tables to public services and opening hours of clinics or shops and hence enforces the perpetuation of unequal opportunities. Due to the lack of child care facilities, young parents fall back into traditional gender roles because they have no other option. The state has an important role in promoting women's rights. It is easier to address institutional deficiencies than to change the mentality of citizens. Hence, the provision of affordable child care could contribute to the transformation of social attitudes.

The vote is another core aspect of the democratic state. Beside the challenge of unequal access to power and resources, the two plebiscites on Swiss women's political rights demonstrate the problem of exclusion. In addition, the struggle for women's rights shows the problematic aspects of the system of direct democracy with its plebiscites on issues beyond elections. Switzerland is proud of its diversity and a political culture of tolerance, consociationalism, and compromise. Nevertheless, outcomes of plebiscites may have a detrimental effect on individuals and groups. Swiss women are an appropriate example.

The introduction of political rights of women did not eliminate all other forms of discrimination. Assertions that women have equal rights and that it is up to women to claim them disregard the complexity of the political, social, and economic context because equal rights do not translate into equal opportunities. There are still unfair differences in terms of political representation of women, equal pay, career opportunities, the burden of care provisions, levels of poverty among women and incidences of violence. Federalism offers opportunities but also has disadvantages. More progressive cantons promoting and implementing women's rights can be used as role models also for the implementation of change on the national level. On the other hand, the considerable autonomy of cantons make it more challenging for women to demand their rights and equal opportunities in conservative cantons.

Finally, the Swiss example not only proves the importance of human rights, dignity, and personal freedoms as non-negotiable foundations of democracy but also demonstrates the limitations of democratic systems. From a human rights perspective, it wouldn't have been necessary to let Swiss men decide on the right of women to vote and participate in politics in order that Switzerland becomes a full democracy. Democracy should be a space of choices and opportunities to pursue one's aspiration in a context of mutual respect, rights and obligations; it should include those with less power and resources. Human rights and personal freedoms do not interfere with democratic rights, on the contrary, they are the safeguards of democracy in a context where democracies have become increasingly vulnerable to be used or undermined by powerful interests. Human rights protect the rights of individuals and limit the destructive potential of the electorate. They are the foundations of democracies and hence are beyond the deliberations and negotiations of daily politics or electoral contestation. The struggle of Swiss women is an appropriate example.

NOTES

1. R. Levy and D. Joye, "Sozialstruktur und Wirtschaftsstruktur," *Handbuch der Schweizer Politik* (Zurich: NZZ Verlag, 2014), 61–62.
2. Frauen and Wahlen, *Bundesamt fur Statistik,* https://www.bfs.admin.ch/bfs/de/home/statistiken/politik/wahlen/frauen.html#1390978129.
3. P. Norris and R. Inglehart, "Cultural Obstacles to Equal Representation," *Journal of Democracy* vol. 12, no. 3 (2001).
4. A. Gouws and H. Kotzé, "Women in Leadership Positions in South Africa: The Role of Values," *Politikon* vol. 34, no. 2 (2007).
5. N. Frazer, "Rethinking Recognition," *New Left Review* no. 3 (May, June 2000).
6. M. Beard, *Women and Power* (London: Profile Books, 2017).
7. M. Harris-Perry, *Sister Citizen* (New Haven: Yale University Press, 2011), 42.
8. Levy and Joye, "Sozialstruktur und Wirtschaftsstruktur," 65–66.
9. Gendering and Mautienne Prod, *Langsam aber sicher! Die politischen Rechte der Schweizer Frauen* (Geneva: Verein Gendering, 2011).
10. T. Held and R. Levy, *Die Stellung der Frau in Familie und Gesellschaft*, 2nd edition (Frauenfeld: Verlag Huber, 1983).
11. Held and Levy, 23–25.
12. Held and Levy, 37.
13. Held and Levy, 57.
14. Held and Levy, 127.
15. Held and Levy, 2. Edition, Frauenfeld: Verlag Huber, 1983, 182–186.
16. Held and Levy, 202–4.
17. Deneys, H. *Bulletin Swiss Parliament*, Postulat 80.353, December 2, 1980, 1369.
18. Eidgenoessische Kommission fuer Frauenfragen, Gewalt an Frauen in der Schweiz, *Frauenfragen* 5 Jahrgang, no. 2 (1982).
19. C. Offe, "Democracy and Trust," *Theoria* no. 96 (December 2000).
20. Volksabstimmung vom 01.02.1959, *Bundeskanzlei* (1959). https://www.bk.admin.ch/ch/d/pore/va/19590201/index.html.
21. Volksabstimmung vom 07.02.1971, *Bundeskanzlei* (1971). https://www.bk.admin.ch/ch/d/pore/va/19710207/index.html.
22. Volksabstimmung vom 14.06.1981, *Bundeskanzlei* (1981). https://www.bk.admin.ch/ch/d/pore/va/19810614/det306.html.
23. Volksabstimmung vom 22.09.1985, *Bundeskanzlei* (1985). https://www.bk.admin.ch/ch/d/pore/va/19850922/index.html.
24. Von Felten, M. "Sexuelle Gewalt in der Ehe als Offizialdelikt," Revision der Artikel 189 und 190, STGB. *Parlamentarische Initiative 96.465* (1996). https://www.parlament.ch/de/ratsbetrieb/suche-curia-vista/geschaeft?AffairId=19960465.
25. Volksabstimmung vom 25.11.2018, *Bundeskanzlei* (2018). https://www.bk.admin.ch/ch/d/pore/va/20181125/det624.html.
26. U. Klöti, Regierung, *Handbuch der Schweizer Politik* (Zurich: NZZ Verlag, 2006), 105.
27. R. Levy, "Wie sich Paare beim Elternwerden retraditionaliseren, und das gegen ihre eigenen Ideale," *Swiss Academies Communication* vol. 11, no. 3 (2016).

REFERENCES

Beard, M. *Women and Power*. London: Profile Books, 2017.
Frauen and Wahlen. *Bundesamt fuer Statistik*, 2015. https://www.bfs.admin.ch/bfs/de/home/statistiken/politik/wahlen/frauen.html#1390978129.
Deneys, H. *Bulletin Swiss Parliament*, Postulat 80.353, December 2, 1980, 1369.
Eidgenoessische Kommission fuer Frauenfragen. "Gewalt an Frauen in der Schweiz." *Frauen-fragen*, 5 Jahrgang, no. 2 (June 1982).
Frazer, N. "Rethinking Recognition." *New Left Review* no. 3 (May, June 2000).
Gendering and Mautienne Prod, *Langsam aber sicher! Die politischen Rechte der Schweizer Frauen*. Geneva: Verein Gendering, 2011.
Gouws, A., and H. Kotzé. "Women in Leadership Positions in South Africa: The Role of Values." *Politikon* vol. 34, no. 2 (2007).
Harris-Perry, M. *Sister Citizen*. New Haven: Yale University Press, 2011.
Held, T. and R. Levy. *Die Stellung der Frau in Familie und Gesellschaft*. Frauenfeld: Verlag Huber, 1974.
Klöti, U., Regierung. *Handbuch der Schweizer Politik*. Zurich: NZZ Verlag, 2006.
Levy, R. and D. Joye, "Sozialstruktur und Wirtschaftsstruktur." *Handbuch der Schweizer Politik*. Zurich, NZZ Verlag, 2014.
Levy, R. "Wie sich Paare beim Elternwerden retraditionaliseren, und das gegen ihre eigenen Ideale." *Swiss Academies Communication* vol. 11, no. 3 (2016).
Norris, P. and R. Inglehart, R. "Cultural Obstacles to Equal Representation." *Journal of Democracy* vol. 12, no. 3 (2001).
Offe, C. "Democracy and Trust." *Theoria* no. 96 (December 2000).
Volksabstimmung vom 01.02.1959, *Bundeskanzlei* (1959). https://www.bk.admin.ch/ch/d/pore/va/19590201/index.html.
Volksabstimmung vom 07.02.1971, *Bundeskanzlei* (1971). https://www.bk.admin.ch/ch/d/pore/va/19710207/index.html.
Volksabstimmung vom 14.06.1981, *Bundeskanzlei* (1981). https://www.bk.admin.ch/ch/d/pore/va/19810614/det306.html.
Volksabstimmung vom 22.09.1985, *Bundeskanzlei* (1985). https://www.bk.admin.ch/ch/d/pore/va/19850922/index.html.
Volksabstimmung vom 25.11.2018, *Bundeskanzlei* (2018). https://www.bk.admin.ch/ch/d/pore/va/20181125/det624.html.
Von Felten, "M. Sexuelle Gewalt in der Ehe als Offizialdelikt. Revision der Artikel 189 und 190 STGB." *Parlamentarische Initiative 96.465* (1996). https://www.parlament.ch/de/ratsbetrieb/suche-curia-vista/geschaeft?AffairId=19960465.

Chapter Five

Ruiz de Burton's Inviolable Californios and Roguish Anglos in *The Squatter and the Don* and *Who Would Have Thought It?*

Geovani Ramirez

María Amparo Ruiz de Burton was born in 1832 to an influential arisatocratic family in Alta California.[1] Ruiz de Burton's political clout, however, would be curtailed by the Anglo-American annexation of Mexico and heavy Anglo-American migration west. The California Gold Rush transformed the region's demographics and political structure. As early as 1849, 100,000 newcomers arrived in California, and 80,000 of those newcomers were Yankees.[2] By the 1850s, Anglo-Americans had wrested control over the region from the Californios. Numbering 7,000 when the US annexed California, the Californios were, as Rodman Paul describes, submerged "beneath the unprecedented flood of [largely Anglo] immigrants that started with the gold rush and continued throughout the rest of the century."[3] This influx culminated in a whopping population of 1.5 million by the end of the nineteenth century.[4]

This submergence of Californios carried over into the economic and political spheres of nineteenth century California life as Anglo-American immigrants "changed pastoral California into a commercial, city-centered, speculative, and money-minded capitalistic economy"[5] and displaced Californio politicians.[6] While in the 1850s people with Spanish surnames served in various local offices, those numbers dwindled by the 1860s and 1870s.[7] Along with their control over California, Anglo-Americans developed nativist attitudes that informed their poor treatment of non-white minorities, including Mexican-heritage subjects.[8] Leonard Pitt informs us that soon after their migration into California, "angry Yankees" lumped all Spanish-speaking people as "interlopers" and "greasers" with no regard for ethnic (or class) differences.[9] The Foreign Miner's Tax Law of 1850, which charged foreign miners a hefty sum to work in the gold mines, targeted Spanish-speaking people and played a large role in their displacement.[10] Nativist Anglo-Americans routinely enforced the law through violence and even murder.[11] The Californios themselves actually left gold mining to Anglo-Americans and other foreigners, but as Pitt observes, "the mines became the staging ground for widespread attacks on their ranchos and pueblos, the rehearsal place for broad-scale assaults on the Spanish-speaking."[12] Pitt's statement alludes to Manifest Destiny and these Anglo-American miners' roles in squatting on Californio lands.

These historical facts inform Ruiz de Burton's novels. By the late nineteenth century, when Ruiz de Burton published *Who Would Have Thought It?* (1872) and *The Squatter and the Don* (1885), the legacy of Manifest Destiny and squatter laws were still affecting landed Mexican-heritage people.[13] Furthermore, monopolizing capitalism threatened to ruin Californios financially as their hacienda systems varied significantly from the capitalist economic market that dominated the second half of the US nineteenth century.[14] Ruiz de Burton's lengthy novels are testaments to her forceful response to these two powerful and transformative forces that (re)defined and (re)shaped national US politics, governing, economics, and national identity and displaced Californios and other Mexican-heritage people in the US Southwest during the second half of the nineteenth century.[15] The roles of didact, sociologist, and historian that Ruiz de Burton carves out for herself through her novels show how critically she experienced her continual disenfranchisement and exemplify her bold engagement in broader national debates.

The cultural and historical work Ruiz de Burton carries out in her novels has strong implications for re-evaluating US history and its national identity and literature. In Alemán's words, Ruiz de Burton's novels "shake to its foundation the American literary tradition and its attendant narrative of nationhood."[16] Ruiz de Burton does so partly by altering the discourse of whiteness in the US. Rather than viewing whiteness as a stable and exclusive Anglo-American racial identity, Ruiz de Burton exposes "whiteness as a construct historically contingent on legal positioning, regional location, and class status."[17] Alemán observes that through depicting the Mexican Lola Medina's pure whiteness in *Who Would Have Thought It?*, Ruiz de Burton offers alternative racial codes that account for "multiple levels of hybrid racial identity" and challenge the US's black/white racial paradigm.[18] Ruiz de Burton's racial re-coding challenges the nativist narrative of an Anglo-American nation in which Anglos reserve the rights to citizenship while excluding other non-Anglo people.[19] Additionally, in *The Squatter and the*

Don Ruiz de Burton historicizes and envisions an empowered Mexican-heritage existence within the geo-political borders of the US that resist her historical realities. Her emphasis on Californios' (Mexican-heritage) natural presence in the US Southwest also resists her contemporary and current Anglo-American nativist narratives that define Mexican-heritage subjects, and Latina/os by extension, as foreigners to the US. Through showing us the process by which Mexican-heritage subjects lost their social status and economic and political power in the US in *The Squatter and the Don*, Ruiz de Burton helps us understand Mexican-heritage marginalization not as a stable form of existence but as a historical, legislative, economic, and political process. Scholars such as Rosaura Sánchez and Beatrice Pita have noted the subversive quality of Ruiz de Burton's work. They celebrate *The Squatter and the Don* as a work that offered "a narrative space for the counter-history of the subaltern" conquered Californios. [20]

Ruiz de Burton's contributions to decolonizing studies, however, are complicated by the semi-feudal, colonialist order that she envisions for a US future and the racist (and classist) logic that accompanies it. José F. Aranda Jr. sums up Ruiz de Burton well when he asserts that Ruiz de Burton is "willing to wage a rhetorical war on her conquerors but also anxious to reassume the privileges of a colonialist." [21] As an Old World colonialist and proponent of a New World colonialism inclusive of Californios, Ruiz de Burton is at odds with historically marginalized minorities. For instance, Ruiz de Burton challenges Anglo-American conceptions of whiteness by expanding whiteness to Californios, but as Jesse Alemán is careful to point out, she does so at the cost of Native Americans and African Americans (and mestizos and Asians) with whom she contrasts Californios as she "constructs the civility of Hispano whiteness." [22] Jennifer Tuttle likewise notes that Ruiz de Burton "allies her Californio protagonists with Anglo Americans and against others of Spanish Mexican descent (particularly those in the working class), belying the *mestizo* status of most Californios." [23]

Ruiz de Burton's colonialist status and attitudes thus distinguish her novels from narratives of resistance most commonly associated with her Mexican-heritage contemporaries, [24] and they trouble the subaltern thesis proposed by Chicana/o scholars such as Rosaura Sánchez and Beatrice Pita. [25] Latina/o studies critics have traditionally been troubled by Ruiz de Burton's racism, privilege, and class as well as her complex political views. [26] Aranda Jr. points out that as late as 2004 "most Chicano/a critics have been reluctant to acknowledge the many paradoxical instances where Ruiz de Burton's political and literary strategies ally her with Anglo American constituencies." [27] Alemán likewise notes Chicana/o scholars' "struggle to resolve the problem of Mexican American whiteness," since "the contradiction between Mexican American dispossession and claims to white citizenship rights remains the thorn in the side of Chicana/o literary history." [28]

Historically, Mexican-heritage elites of the US Southwest embraced their ostensibly pure European cultural and racial backgrounds to distinguish themselves from Native American and Mexican mestizo workers prior to and after the treaty of Guadalupe Hidalgo.[29] Ruiz de Burton herself was a confederate sympathizer, and, as a landed Californiana, held dehumanizing views toward Native American people.[30] What is more, Ruiz de Burton married US Captain Henry S. Burton, a soldier of the conquering Yankee army, who was in charge of suppressing Native American rebellions.[31] Her marriage to Burton, then, not only "endowed her with social mobility," as Julie Ruiz suggests, but also aligned her with an officer who had played a direct role in a US military campaign into California.[32] In fact, as Sánchez and Pita note, Lieutenant-Colonel "Burton's expeditionary forces were the first to occupy any area of Baja California."[33]

Though potentially troubling, Ruiz de Burton's contradictory positionalities to colonialism help us gain a more comprehensive understanding of Mexican-heritage subjects' (literary) histories within the US. Beyond that, Ruiz de Burton's work has, in Amelia María de la Luz Montes and Anne Elizabeth Goldman's words, contributed to the "reconfiguration of nineteenth-century American literary culture more generally."[34] The collective essays in *María Amparo Ruiz de Burton: Critical and Pedagogical Perspectives* (2004) take for granted Ruiz de Burton's complexity and, in the editors' words, "appraise a politically complex Mexican American writer alternately celebrated as marginalized and censured as a snob."[35] These essays furthermore "articulate the contradictions of colonial identity in California."[36] My work likewise continues to explore the ways through which Ruiz de Burton positions herself as an increasingly marginalized but Old World colonial subject. I diverge from these previous scholars, however, in showing that Ruiz de Burton ultimately makes claims in both of her novels for the superiority of aristocratic Mexican-heritage subjects over *all* Anglo-Americans without any distinction to class or occupation.

I concede that through marriage plots between Mexican-heritage aristocrats and Anglo-American elites in both her novels, Ruiz de Burton envisions what Josef Raab calls an elite "inter-ethnic and inter-American community" based on "shared values and ideologies."[37] Certainly, by depicting Californios as white aristocrats, capable of adapting to the economic demands of modernization, Ruiz de Burton conflates Californios with Anglo-Americans and ingratiates Californios with her predominantly Anglo-American audience.[38] However, I suggest that more than reflecting a desire to create a simple elite Mexican-heritage/Anglo union, Ruiz de Burton disidentifies with Anglo-Americans, neither fully rejecting nor embracing them, to regain socioeconomic and political control for Californios in the US.

I argue that Ruiz de Burton *disidentifies* with Anglo-Americans to promote a narrative of a white, culturally refined, and morally superior Mexican-heritage aristocratic class best fit to rule in the US Southwest. Ruiz de Burton's emphasis on the cultural and moral superiority of Mexican-heritage aristocratic subjects over Anglos is a form of disidentification with colonialist logics. Combining Eve Kosofsky Sedgwick's theory on identification, which suggests identification always involves "counteridentifying," and Kimberlé Crenshaw's theory of intersectionality, José Esteban Muñoz proposes a theory of disidentification that involves neither assimilating within a dominant ideology "nor strictly oppos[ing] it."[39] This act and process of disidentifying then serves decolonizing purposes by transforming hegemonic models from within, though such transformation does not necessarily ensure universal human rights. As John Morán González notes, Ruiz de Burton's *The Squatter and the Don*'s narrative "outlines the limitations and inadequacies of appropriating national allegory for interpretive projects of dismantling colonial difference."[40] Morán Gonzalez's assessment of Ruiz de Burton's reification of whiteness by depicting Mexican whiteness gestures toward Ruiz de Burton's racial and colonial disidentification with Anglo-Americans.[41] Other scholars such as Jesse Alemán similarly note Ruiz de Burton's racial and colonial disidentification when he observes that her cultural work "challenges the Anglocentricism of Northeastern America by arguing that upper-class Californios are white."[42] Likewise, Rosaura Sánchez and Beatrice Pita account for Ruiz de Burton's disidentification with Anglo-Americans in their introduction to *Conflicts of Interest: The Letters of María Amparo Ruiz de Burton* (2001) despite having proposed the subaltern thesis in their introduction to *The Squatter and the Don* (1992). They even use the term explicitly when they acknowledge Ruiz de Burton's "contradictory accommodation to and disidentification with the United States" (xvi).[43] Though their use of the term suggests they understand disidentification as an act or process of resisting (as contrasted to "accommodation"), their awareness of Ruiz de Burton's incorporation of both "accommodation" and "disidentification" amounts to my understanding of disidentification as neither fully embracing nor rejecting. Their reading of Ruiz de Burton, like mine, accounts for Ruiz de Burton's shifts in rhetorical moves depending on her political agendas. They note, for instance, that Ruiz de Burton was able to "shift or maneuver from one position to another, allowing expediency and convenience to determine her course of action and opinion in order to gain relative ground or secure some advantage, however tentatively."[44] While I agree with Sánchez and Pita that Ruiz de Burton was at times opportunistic, I suggest that her aristocratic elitism never leaves that opportunism, so that her depictions of Anglo-Americans, regardless of class or occupation, always cast Anglo-Americans as generally inferior culturally and morally to aristocratic Mexican-heritage subjects.

In a reversal of the Spanish figure that María DeGuzmán traces in anti-Spanish Anglo-American imperialistic rhetoric, Ruiz de Burton depicts Mex-

ican-heritage subjects in overwhelmingly superior ways, culturally and morally, to unlawful Anglo-American squatters in *The Squatter and the Don* and
corrupt politicians in both novels. Anglo-Americans prior to, during, and
after the nineteenth century racialized Spaniards and conflated Spanish
swarthiness with moral darkness, constructing an Anglo-American Protestant
national identity based on the constructed racial, and therefore moral, distinctions between Anglos and Spaniards.[45] Ruiz de Burton would have been
familiar with this kind of racialized othering of Spaniards (and Californios),
and she rejects these Anglo-American narratives of Spanish off-whiteness by
shedding them and re-casting them onto Anglo-Americans.[46] In *Who Would
Have Thought It?*, the Mexican Lola is of Austrian descent and phenotypical-
ly white as Northern Protestants but morally purer. In *The Squatter and the
Don*, the Alamar men are said to resemble Englishmen while also demonstrating more refinement and higher morals than their Anglo-American
counterparts. Thus, I argue that Ruiz de Burton attempts to re-store Californios to their proper socioeconomic and political positions not only based on
their white race, but by virtue of their aristocratic background.[47]

For Ruiz de Burton, a Californio integration into US society relies heavily
on her narratives of a Californio aristocracy and a virtually monolithic politically and economically rising but morally declining Anglo working class. In
both novels, the narrators elevate Californios above working class Anglo-
Americans based on those differences and the integrity and moral compasses
that ostensibly define their particular classes. Karen Kilcup observes that in
The Squatter and the Don, "Squatters appear in an almost uniformly negative
light, as types of savages" and are depicted as "Immoral, uneducated, greedy,
and illiterate."[48] Likewise, in *Who Would Have Thought It?* Ruiz de Burton
depicts the majority of affluent and influential Anglo-American characters,
most of them politicians and/or businessmen, as corrupt to critique their
positions of power and affluence. She also emphasizes some of their working
class backgrounds to suggest that they owe their low moral principles and
lack of values partly to their working class backgrounds. Furthermore, I
argue that Ruiz de Burton exploits conservative notions about women's religious and sexual purity to promote her narrative about Californios' moral and
cultural superiority over Anglo-Americans. This rhetorical move underscores
the cultural and moral values that Californios would bring into what Ruiz de
Burton presents as a morally and culturally deficient nineteenth century Anglo US nation.

I will first discuss the climactic clash between the Don, the epitome of
culture and reason, and Mr. Darrell, a squatter and morally ambiguous man,
to illustrate the stark differences in refinement and morality that Ruiz de
Burton delineates between Californios and Anglo squatters. The confronta-
tion occurs when the Don and Mr. Darrell meet during the Don's cattle drive.
In his greeting, the Don pleasantly and respectfully addresses Darrell as "Mr.

Darrell." The Don also playfully says to Mr. Darrell during the exchange, "*You see* we are Clarence's vaqueros now."[49] Actually, the Don has sold his cattle to Mr. Darrell's son Clarence to prevent more of his cattle from being killed by squatters.

We see that this encounter and the Don's words are packed with irony when we consider the context of the novel and Ruiz de Burton's incessant critique of squatting and the laws that protect the Anglos' land appropriation and economic exploitation of the Californio landowners. The narrator refers to the squatter as Darrell in this scene while referring to Don Mariano as "the Don," an authorial choice that highlights the class differences between the aristocrat Don Mariano and the working-class squatter Darrell. The two men's actions during this meeting further emphasize their class differences. The Don, the epitome of "aristocratic virtue," as Timothy Deines notes, responds gracefully to his unfortunate socioeconomic and political circumstances, including in this moment when he respectfully addresses Mr. Darrell though Darrell threatens his lands. Mr. Darrell, on the other hand, insults and challenges the Don to a physical fight.[50] Melanie Dawson suggests that the Don "exemplifies his role as one of the gente de razón, or 'people of reason' rather than a man controlled by his emotional state."[51] The Don's equanimity is a stark contrast to that of Mr. Darrell who in this same interaction accuses the Don of prostituting his daughter to Clarence and becomes "angry" and "enraged."[52] Mr. Darrell also mutters and gasps from his anger, unable to speak like a human being.[53]

Part of Ruiz de Burton's methods toward integrating Mexican-heritage aristocrats into the US fabric, I would argue, relies on showing what is lost in the process of transforming California into an Anglo-American dominated and monopolized territory. Dawson calls our attention to how the "acquisitory passions that Americans claim as their right" lead to a "fading away of [a Californio] life," defined by an agrarian economy.[54] Jennifer Tuttle signals to Californios' and the region's loss of health when she asserts that Ruiz de Burton marks squatters and "corrupt lawyers, judges, legislators and railroad monopolists . . . as malignant forces that contaminate the region and sicken its 'native' inhabitants."[55] I would add that Ruiz de Burton also shows that civility and reason are lost as the Californio way of life fades. Referencing Herbert Spencer in *The Squatter and the Don* on multiple occasions, we can imagine Ruiz de Burton appropriating more than his survival of the fittest concept. Spencer warned that "if we were controlled by surges of emotion . . . then we would slip away from the modern world" into a primal one.[56] He therefore urged human beings "to be self-restrained" and "balanced" when making choices and taking actions.[57] Ruiz de Burton has us believe that the restraint and decorum of the aristocratic Don Mariano would enable him (and other Californios) to make fair and level-headed political and economic decisions if they were politically empowered. By showing the

Don's refinement and kindness during particularly adverse times, Ruiz de Burton dramatizes the cultural (and moral) practices lost within the geo-political spheres of the US southwest through the displacement of Mexican-heritage aristocrats.

Ruiz de Burton similarly contrasts Californios with the Anglo-American elite in *Who Would Have Thought It?* where the Cackles, working class men who have risen politically and economically through a combination of char-ity, happy accidents, corruption, and nepotism, represent the "unworthy" Anglo-American elite and ruling classes.[58] The narrator observes that the Cackles, whose name emphasizes their coarseness, "march in front of the rank, leading the American people shoulder to shoulder" with other morally corrupt characters.[59] We also learn that Congressmen Beau and Tool Cackle "were making money as fast as if by magic" and that "the brothers had got several Government contracts, in other persons' names, by which they made enormous profits."[60] On the surface, these Cackles join the long list of other corrupt US Anglo-American politicians in Ruiz de Burton's novels, and their self-serving misgoverning is yet another critique of an Anglo-American So-cially Darwinian approach toward leadership, community, and economics.

However, Ruiz de Burton also mocks these Cackles based on their class. She presents the Cackles, as previously-working-class, unrefined, wealthy politicians, to show that working class and elite Anglo-Americans are cultu-rally and morally indistinguishable: "Mr. Cackle, the father, dressed in the finest broadcloth, resting his yet firm hand upon a gold-headed cane, sat on a velvet-cushioned chair by the library centre-table of the Cackle mansion at Washington."[61] The passage reveals the narrator's (and Ruiz de Burton's) ethnically tied class prejudices. In the passage, the narrator is overwhelming-ly more preoccupied with the Cackles' working-class background and coarseness than their corruption. The details about the Cackles' ostentatious-ness comments on their excessive and crass enjoyment of luxuries and em-phasizes their unnatural presence within a luxurious environment. Ruiz de Burton, then, uses the Cackles to illustrate the relationship between Anglo-Americans' poor breeding and their immoral principles. Caesar Cackle ad-mits to "hat[ing] poverty" and assures us he "wouldn't for the world" return to the farm labor he carried out prior to becoming a politician.[62] His brother Beau later urges his fellow Cackles that "by fair or foul means the Cackles must hold to their power."[63] Ruiz de Burton here exposes the common self-serving machinations of Anglo legislators and other officials driven by spe-cial economic and political interests. By conflating morality and class, Ruiz de Burton argues that the Cackles are as culturally and morally unfit to rule as they are unfit to enjoy the luxuries they have acquired through immoral means. While the Cackles are unfit to reside in their mansions and govern the US, the aristocratic Californios are, by comparison, naturally suited to higher social stations and positions of power in the US.

These comparisons also play out in the moral distinctions Ruiz de Burton draws between Mexican-heritage Catholic and Anglo-American Protestant women. I argue that Ruiz de Burton adheres to patriarchal gender norms in her depiction of women as a way to re-enforce her claims about the moral and cultural superiority of aristocratic Mexican-heritage subjects over Anglo-Americans. In *Who Would Have Thought It?* Ruiz de Burton contrasts the two matriarchal representatives of the Mexican-heritage aristocracy and pseudo Anglo-American bourgeoisie, Doña Theresa, and Mrs. Norval, respectively.

Ruiz de Burton's heavy-handed depiction of Mrs. Norval, a strict Protestant religious hypocrite and social climber, exposes the wide gap in refinement and morality that Ruiz de Burton insists exists between aristocratic Mexican-heritage Catholics and Anglo Protestants. Citing Amy Kaplan's work on "manifest domesticity," in which Anglo women identified with their male counterparts against non-Anglo-Americans and worked to domesticate foreigners in the interest of the US nation, Julie Ruiz discusses Ruiz de Burton's depiction of women in *Who Would Have Thought It?* as metaphors for their nation,[64] suggesting that Mrs. Norval "simultaneously extends the imperializing reach of influence as her 'Christian' duty" through using young Lola's wealth "while constantly fearing contagion from that 'uncivilized' child [Lola] she must domesticate."[65] Ruiz ultimately shows how Ruiz de Burton inverts this relationship with full force, depicting Mrs. Norval as a "savage" and Lola her civilized victim (thereby drawing a relationship between Mrs. Norval and the Native people who captured Lola's mother, Doña Theresa).[66] I too focus on Ruiz de Burton's depiction of Mrs. Norval's inherent inferiority to Mexican-heritage women, but I do so through comparing Mrs. Norval to Doña Theresa, and I suggest that Ruiz de Burton subordinates gender under class concerns in her attempt to depict Mexican-heritage aristocratic subjects as more fit to govern in the US than Anglo-Americans.

From our first introduction to Mrs. Norval we see her lack of refinement through her excessive emotionality. When her husband arrives from a trip with a "black" child (Lola) whom he has adopted, Mrs. Norval is insufferable. She holds a teapot "with a look that suggested a wish on her part to welcome her husband by throwing it at his devoted head."[67] What is more, when told that the child will join the family, "Mrs. Norval's hand shook so violently on hearing this that she poured the tea all over the tray."[68] She was afterward "too angry to speak," and only a few moments later "suppressed a groan."[69] In only a few more instances, "Mrs. Norval had utterly lost patience," and in yet a few more moments, "Mrs. Norval bit her lip" and "could almost have cried with vexation" to have this child in her home.[70] Through these depictions of Mrs. Norval's cruelty and intense emotions, reminiscent of Mr. Darrell the squatter, Ruiz de Burton represents Mrs. Norval's lack of cultural refinement and her deficient moral compass. In this scene, the narrative shows us that Mrs. Norval is an inhospitable, crude, violent, unstable, beastly creature. Ruiz identifies a similar lack of civility and refinement in Mrs. Norval's crude "loss of self-control and restraint" in her visceral responses to and greed over Lola's inherited riches.[71]

Moreover, this same cold, rigid Mrs. Norval later thaws or, from the narrative's perspective, overheats in a way that compounds her moral deficiency and that unravels Protestant ideals of chastity. When Mr. Norval is presumed dead, Mrs. Norval soon awakens to her sexual desires for the Reverend Mr. Hackwell. We are told "She felt a thrill through her entire frame, just as might have felt one of those creatures—whom she abhorred—who go to parties in low necks and short sleeves, and . . . in their wild chase after worldly pleasures, do court such thrills."[72] In fact, she, "a pious, proper churchwoman, felt just the same" and feels not shock but pleasure at finding herself in this "antithetical position with her former self," in feeling her "heart throbbing in such unmatronly, unpresbyterian tumult."[73] The narrator adds, "'Oh, John! you have such power over me!' sighed the mature inamorata."[74] Further, the narrator comments, "it would have been better, perhaps, that . . . Mrs. Norval's heart had never thawed. . . . She had so far degenerated that she regarded her youth as misspent, her life a blank, until she loved Hackwell, until she was past forty."[75] The combination of the narrator's critical interjections and commentary on the dissolute transformation, thoughts, and desires of Mrs. Norval intensify the severity of Mrs. Norval's presumed transgressions, and they also mock Mrs. Norval on religious, ageist, and gendered terms. She is too old for these sentiments, the narrator has us believe, and what is more, through her hypocrisy we see her religious principles, and Protestantism more generally, crumbling. There are no distinctions, then, for Ruiz de Burton, between those wild "creatures" and this "pious, proper [Protestant] churchwoman."[76]

Predictably, Ruiz de Burton contrasts the downfallen Mrs. Norval with Doña Theresa, a chaste Mexican-heritage aristocratic woman who was captured by Native Americans, forced to marry the chief, and lived among them until, presumably, she suffered an untimely death as a result of her life among her Native captors. We learn about her first through Dr. Norval, a geologist and physician who fortuitously met her and her young daughter, Lolita, when he entered their village to help treat the chief and his two sons. Doña Theresa pleads with Dr. Norval "for the love of God, and for humanity's sake"[77] to take Lolita with him on his departure, and she offers him her vast treasure of gold nuggets to persuade him.[78] Dr. Norval agrees to do so, and he observes that as they neared their departure "Doña Theresa herself was visibly declining in health, and daily becoming more weak and emaciated," attributing her quick death to the loss of her daughter.[79] However, Doña Theresa's narrative tells a different story, one that reveals her colonialist, classist, and racist views about Native people and that suggests she died from her exposure to them. Thus, as Ruiz helps us see, Ruiz de Burton simultaneously aligns Mrs. Norval and New England Protestantism with savagery while recuperating "Old World Spanish Catholicism"[80] from stereotypes that otherwise pair Native people and Catholicism as primitive, superstitious, and irrational.[81]

We learn a bit about Doña Theresa's character and how she experienced her life among Native people when Don Luis, her husband, reads a letter she dictated to a stenographer named Lebrun as she was dying. In that letter, Doña Theresa discloses details that suggest she died from having been exposed to a toxic Native American environment for which she is unfit. "At this hour of my death, . . . and when about to appear before my Maker," she begins, "I forgive the horrible savages who inflicted upon me the most terrible torture that the human soul can know,—the agony of living in degradation forever on earth."[82] Tuttle's insightful argument that Ruiz de Burton uses discourses of nervousness to mark her Californio characters "as both genteel and white" illuminates the racial and class distinctions Doña Theresa draws between herself and the Native people among whom she lived.[83]

According to Tuttle, late nineteenth century medical rhetoric linked illness and nervousness with class and race.[84] Women, in particular, were read in this manner so that "women of color and working-class women, who generally were viewed as 'uncivilized' and therefore naturally healthy, [and] less refined" were thought "immune to suffering and well suited for lives of labor."[85] Wealthy Anglo-American women, on the other hand, were thought hypersensitive so that "Their inherently delicate and excitable nervous systems would break down from the slightest mental, physical, or emotional strain."[86] As a result of this racialized and classed medical rhetoric surrounding nervousness, there "was a profusion of pale, nervous, swooning, and dying white heroines in fiction from this period who represented a leisured, race-coded, highly romanticized model of invalid womanhood."[87] Doña Theresa is yet another one of these refined, wealthy, white women to fall ill from mental and emotional strain, and thus we can see how Ruiz de Burton is borrowing from this medical rhetoric to emphasize Doña Theresa's whiteness and aristocracy.[88]

Ruiz de Burton wishes to show us that, as an aristocratic Mexican-heritage subject of European stock, Doña Theresa was unfit, too refined to exist among the crude Native people and their primitive lifestyles. Doña Theresa's strong words ("terrible torture" and "agony") to describe her life among the Native Americans highlight the detrimental emotional and mental effects that living among her Native captors has caused her as well as her displeasure for enduring that. Her untimely death, we might surmise by her letter, can be traced to the "degradation" she has experienced among the Native people. On the one hand, we can reasonably assume that Doña Theresa resents and is repelled by the Native American people because they abducted her. She was, after all, forced into marriage with the chief. However, her references to Native people in her letter suggest that she was as repelled by them as much by their race and culture as by their abduction of her. Her description of them as "horrible savages" marks a strong contrast between herself and them based on racializing colonialist logics that cast Native American people as subhuman and Europeans as civilized human beings. Her words echo Mr. Hackwell's distinction between what he refers to as *"the natives"* of California comprised "mostly of Spanish descent" and the cannibalistic "Wild Indians of Colorado" toward the opening of the novel.[89] Indeed, as Alemán points out, "the novel goes to great lengths . . . to show . . . that 'the natives' of Spanish descent, as the narrative often describes them, are not at all like those 'horrid' Indians or Mexicans."[90]

Doña Theresa's suggestion that she has suffered "the most terrible torture" and "degradation," then, refers partly to her having had to exist among these people so racially and culturally different from and inferior to herself. She does not offer specifics about what makes these people "horrible savages," a phrase she uses more than once to describe them, but Dr. Norval's observations about their interactions with them suggest that the Native people treat her with respect and kindness.[91] Dr. Norval tells Mrs. Norval that during his first encounter with Doña Theresa, he observed that "The chief . . . seemed to feel the greatest respect for the *ña Hala* [Doña Theresa] (which, in the language of these Indians, means *my lady*), and all the Indians the same, obeying her slightest wish."[92] He also mentions the presence of an "Indian woman so devoted" to Doña Theresa.[93] The Doña, then, has enjoyed a great degree of power, respect, and affection among the Native people in this land. In fact, as Alemán points out, through enjoying the luxury of having the Native people bring her precious stones and selecting only the "largest" and "most perfect" among them,[94] the Doña enacts "in miniature the history of Spanish colonization of the Americas," using "the wealth she gains from indigenous exploitation to rescue (*sacar*) Lola from the threat of Indian identity."[95] In other words, Doña Theresa is only willing to relate with the Native people as their Doña. She is unwilling to acknowledge their shared spaces, for as Dr. Norval observed, the place in which Doña Theresa lay dying was "a miserable Indian hut" where "The surroundings were cheerless enough to kill any civilized woman."[96] She is likewise unwilling for Lola to embrace the Native world that surrounds them, protecting her daughter from partaking in sexual relations with Native people and saving her from Native spirituality through her insistence to Dr. Norval that Lola be raised in her Catholic faith.[97]

The torture of remaining among those "horrid" people, Ruiz de Burton wants us to believe, is an intolerable and impossible task from which Doña Theresa's dying body frees her. Despite, however, what she perceives as her dire and life-threatening circumstances among the Native "savages" (in addition to making her physically ill, the circumstances make her contemplate suicide), Doña Theresa shows an exceptional ability to retain her equanimity and religious principles.[98] As with Don Mariano in *The Squatter and the Don*, we see Doña Theresa respond with the utmost civility and equanimity even within the most dire of circumstances, in this case as she is dying in a wretched place and among "horrible savages." Her ability to "forgive" her torturers, furthermore, exemplifies her strong commitment to her religious principles, which she hints at when she refers to meeting her God, her "Maker." The letter also shows Doña Theresa's spiritual and sexual purity.

The letter's words, as the narrator would have us believe, reveal Doña Theresa's inviolability. Don Luis (and the narrator) recall(s) her as "the pure, the high-minded, refined, and delicate Theresa."[99] In this description we see the mixture of class and morality, the lady's refined character tied to her purity. Ruiz de Burton supports this aristocratic holiness and chastity when as Doña Theresa's husband and father stare at her portrait, the narrator observes, "The beautiful radiant face smiled on them as if saying, 'Do not weep for me. Do not mourn. I am an angel now. I was always pure, for my soul did not sin . . . I was a martyr, now an angel."[100] This free indirect discourse, which simultaneously grants us access into the narrator's, Don Luis', and Don Felipe's views of the chaste Doña Theresa, functions as a counterpoint to the narrator's mocking representation of Mrs. Norval's sexual awakening. The narrator partakes in the approving male gaze upon Doña Theresa's literal and figurative image and re-enforces the patriarchal value of male approval for women's behaviors, which encompasses an implicit critique of female sexuality. Though these men weep over Doña Theresa, they weep over the gendered impurity implicit in her captivity. Don Luis reflects, "She, the pure, the high-minded, refined, and delicate Theresa, to meet such a fate!"[101] For Don Luis, the greatest injustice against Doña Theresa lies in the irony of her defiled chastity. Ruiz de Burton's juxtaposition of gendered Catholicism and Protestantism reminds readers of the Christian values from which the Anglo-American Protestants have strayed and casts Catholic Californios as moral redeemers.

Ruiz de Burton's intense focus on morality is not simply intended to criticize Anglo-Protestantism and its role in promoting Manifest Destiny. More importantly, as Ruiz de Burton pushes for an Anglo-Californio alliance based on commonalities that include whiteness and class, I would add that she pushes for an alliance based on the moral and religious soundness that Californios would bring to such a marriage. In this sense, Californios offer a cure for Anglo-American ills, a potential purification that could help the US nation grow stronger morally, economically, socially (based on standards of refinement), and politically as it continues to expand. Ruiz de Burton moralizes about the destructive effects of Social Darwinism on social structures and moral and religious values to make a case for Californio control over the local economies, politics, and culture, and her rhetoric pushes for a stabilization of class, which would benefit the aristocratic Californios. Furthermore, she shows that Californios, contrary to popular Anglo beliefs, are not impediments to the US' development but rather are vital to the US' healing and progress as a nation through their intact Christian, albeit Catholic, values, refinement, and sense of moral justice and equanimity.

NOTES

1. Jose Aranda Jr., "Contradictory Impulses María Amparo Ruiz de Burton, Resistance Theory, and the Politics of Chicano/a Studies." *American Literature* 70, no. 3 (1998): 556.

2. Leonard Pitt, *The Decline of the Californios: A Social History of the Spanish-Speaking Californias: 1846–1890* (Berkeley, CA: University of California Press, 1966), 52–53.

3. Paul, Rodman W., *The Far West and the Great Plains in Transition, 1859–1900*. 2nd ed. (Norman, OK: University of Oklahoma Press, 1988), 148.

4. Paul, 148.

5. Paul, 148

6. Paul, 149.

7. Paul, 149.

8. Paul, 125.

9. Pitt, *The Decline of Californios*, 53.

10. Paul, *The Far West*, 60–64.

11. Paul, 60–64 and Pitt, *The Decline of Californios*, 62–64. According to Pitt, Anglo-Americans also failed to respect the rights of those Latin-American people (including Mexican-heritage people) with permits, however.

12. Paul, *The Far West*, 55.

13. Ruiz de Burton herself litigated over her Jamul Ranch from shortly after her husband's death in 1869 until 1889. See Aranda Jr's "Contradictory Impulses," 557.

14. Paul, *The Far West*, 148–49.

15. Plenty of other Mexican-heritage writers denounced the US' imperialistic disenfranchisement of Mexican-heritage subjects, but their writings on the subject were neither as extensive nor as nuanced as Ruiz de Burton's. For some examples of these kinds of writings, see Francisco P. Ramírez's "Editorial, July 24, 1885" and "Inquisition" published in *El Clamor Publico*; Pablo de la Guerra's "The Californios" published in *El Clamor Público* in 1856; and, Juan Nepomuceno Cortina's "Proclamation" of 1859, all of which can be found in *Herencia: The Anthology of Hispanic Literature of the United States (Recovering the U.S. Hispanic Literary Heritage)*.

16. Jesse Alemán, "Citizenship Rights and Colonial Whites: The Cultural Work of María Amparo Ruiz de Burton's Novels." In *Complicating Constructions: Race, Ethnicity, and Hybridity in American Texts*, edited by David S. Goldstein and Audrey B. Thacker, 3–30 (Seattle: University of Washington Press, 2007, 4.

17. Alemán, 5.

18. Alemán, 10.

19. Historically speaking, Ruiz de Burton's claims to Californio whiteness would fall on deaf ears. Anglo-American darkening of Spaniards was integral to justifying the US' imperial expansion. See María DeGuzmán's *Spain's Long Shadow*, xxviii. As María DeGuzmán argues, "Anglo-Americans created a fantasy of racial purity through the representations of Spaniards as figures of morally blackened alien whiteness or off-whiteness and doomed hybridity" (xxiv). These historical realities did not discourage Ruiz de Burton from privileging whiteness or convince her of joining forces with other marginalized people.

20. Rosaura Sánchez and Beatrice Pita. Introduction to *Conflicts of Interest: The Letters of María Amparo Ruiz de Burton*, edited by Rosaura Sánchez and Beatrice Pita, ix-xxii (Houston: Arte Público Press, 2001), Introduction to *The Squatter*, 7.

21. Aranda Jr., "Contradictory Impulses," 554.

22. Alemán, 16. In "Thank God, Lolita," 99, Alemán includes Irish people on this list of marginalized people who "remain on the racialized margins of white Mexican privilege."

23. Jennifer S. Tuttle, "The Symptoms of Conquest: Race, Class, and the Nervous Body in *The Squatter and the Don.*" In *María Amparo Ruiz de Burton: Critical and Pedagogical Perspectives*, edited by Amelia María de la Luz Montes and Anne Elizabeth Goldman (New York: Palgrave, 2004), 63.

24. Shimberlee Jión-King, "Breaking the Silence: Contesting Manifest Destiny in María Amparo Ruiz de Burton's Who Would Have Thought It?" *Mester*, 37 (2008): 20–21.

25. See Alemán's "Thank God, Lolita," 97, and Aranda Jr.'s "Returning California to the People," 12–13.

26. For more information on this conversation, see, e.g., Josef Raab's "The Imagined Inter-American Community of María Amparo Ruiz de Burton," José Aranda's "Contradictory Impulses: María Amaparo Ruiz de Burton, Resistance Theory, and the Politics of Chicano/a Studies," and Shimberlee Jión-King's "Breaking the Silence: Contesting Manifest Destiny in María Amparo Ruiz de Burton's *Who Would Have Thought It?*"

27. Aranda Jr., "Returning California to the People," 11.

28. Alemán, "Thank God, Lolita," 97.

29. John Morán Gonzalez, *The Troubled Union: Expansionist Imperatives in Post-Reconstruction American Novels* (Columbus: Ohio State University Press, 2010), 87.

30. Vincent Pérez, *Remembering the Hacienda: History and Memory in the Mexican American Southwest* (College Station, TX: Texas A&M University Press, 2006), 66, 83.

31. Alemán, "Citizenship Rights and Colonial Whites," 4. Marriages between elite Mexican-heritage subjects and Anglos occurred toward the beginning of the Anglo migration westward. For more on this history, see Elisa Warford's "'An Eloquent and Impassioned Plea': The Rhetoric of Ruiz de Burton's *The Squatter and the Don*," 10.

32. Julie Ruiz, "Captive Identities: The Gendered Conquest of Mexico in *Who Would Have Thought It?*" In *María Amparo Ruiz de Burton: Critical and Pedagogical Perspectives*, edited by Amelia María de la Luz Montes and Anne Elizabeth Goldman, 112–32 (New York: Palgrave, 2004), 114.

33. Sánchez and Pita. Introduction to *Conflicts of Interest*, 2.

34. Amelia Maria De la Luz Montes and Anne Elizabeth Goldman, eds. *María Amparo Ruiz de Burton: Critical and Pedagogical Perspectives* (New York: Palgrave, 2004), 1.

35. De la Montes and Goldman, 5.

36. De la Montes and Goldman, 6.

37. Josef Raab, "The Imagined Inter-American Community of María Amparo Ruiz de Burton," *Amerikastudien* 53 (2008): 78.

38. Elisa Warford, "'An Eloquent and Impassioned Plea': The Rhetoric of Ruiz de Burton's *The Squatter and the Don*," *Western American Literature* 44 (2009): 5–21.8–9.

39. Muñoz, José Esteban. *Disidentifications: Queers of Color and the Performance of Politics* (Minneapolis, MN: University of Minnesota Press, 1999), 8, 11–12.

40. Morán Gonzalez, *Troubled Union*, 88.

41. Morán Gonzalez, 87.

42. Alemán, Jesse. "Citizenship Rights and Colonial Whites: The Cultural Work of María Amparo Ruiz de Burton's Novels." In *Complicating Constructions: Race, Ethnicity, and Hybridity in American Texts*, edited by David S. Goldstein and Audrey B. Thacker, 3–30 (Seattle: University of Washington Press, 2007), 5.

43. Sánchez and Pita. Introduction to *Conflicts of Interest*, xvi.

44. Sánchez and Pita, x.

45. DeGuzmán, María. *Spain's Long Shadow: The Black Legend, Off-Whiteness and Anglo-American Empire (*Minneapolis, MN: University of Minnesota Press, 2005), xxiv.

46. DeGuzman, xxiv.

47. Some critics have noted Ruiz de Burton's reification of the racial hierarchy that privileges whiteness. See, e.g., John Morán González's "Blushing Brides and Soulless Corporations" in *The Troubled Union* and Jesse Alemán's "Citizenship Rights and Colonial Whites."

48. Karen L. Kilcup, "Writing Against Wilderness: María Amparo Ruiz de Burton's Elite Environmental Justice," *Western American Literature* 47 (2013): 376.

49. Ruiz de Burton, *The Squatter*, 227.

50. Timothy Deines, "Interrogating the Moral Contract in Ruiz de Burton's *The Squatter and the Don." The Yearbook of Research in English and American Literature* 22 (2006): 271. Mr. Darrell's son Clarence paid the Don for the land upon which Mr. Darrell has been squatting. Now Mr. Darrell goes as far as to suggest that the Don prostituted his own daughter in order to bargain such a payment with Clarence. He further insults the Don in this scene by calling him a coward.

51. Melanie V. Dawson, "Ruiz de Burton's Emotional Landscape: Property and Feeling in *The Squatter and the Don," Nineteenth-Century Literature* 63, no. 1 (2008): 45.

52. Ruiz de Burton, *The Squatter*, 227.

53. Ruiz de Burton, 227.

54. Dawson, "Ruiz de Burton's Emotional Landscape," 44.

55. Tuttle, "Symptoms of Conquest," 56–72. To be clear, Tuttle understands Ruiz de Burton's depiction of Californio illness as an indictment of the aggressive Anglo-American sociopolitical and economic displacement of Californios. However, her main argument revolves around Ruiz de Burton's appropriation of medical theories of illness that linked illness to affluent, white subjects to construct a white aristocratic Mexican-heritage class. See 70–71.

56. Francis, Mark. *Herbert Spencer and the Invention of Modern Life* (London: Routledge Press, 2014), 19.

57. Francis, 33.

58. There are instances in the novel where the narrator makes allusions to the Cackles' economic indebtedness to various characters, including Dr. Norval and Isaac Sprig.

59. Ruiz de Burton, *Who Would Have Thought It?*, 299. Among these morally deficient politicians walks the "Honorable Le Grand Gunn," who uses his authority to keep an innocent love rival imprisoned.

60. Ruiz de Burton, 68.

61. Ruiz de Burton, 294.

62. Ruiz de Burton, 294.

63. Ruiz de Burton, 302.

64. Ruiz, "Captive Identities," 119–28.

65. Ruiz, 119–28.

66. Ruiz, 126.

67. Ruiz de Burton, María Amparo, *Who Would Have Thought It?*, edited by Amelia María de la Luz Montes (New York: Penguin, 2009), 11.

68. Ruiz de Burton, 11.

69. Ruiz de Burton, 12.

70. Ruiz de Burton, 12, 13.

71. Ruiz, "Captive Identities," 121.

72. Ruiz de Burton, *Who Would Have Thought It?*, 171.

73. Ruiz de Burton, 171.

74. Ruiz de Burton, 171.

75. Ruiz de Burton, 171.

76. Ruiz de Burton, 171.

77. In Ruiz de Burton, 28.

78. Ruiz de Burton, 27–29.

79. Ruiz de Burton, 29.

80. Ruiz, "Captive Identities," 122.

81. Ruiz.

82. Ruiz de Burton, *Who Would Have Thought It?*, 201.

83. Tuttle, "Symptoms of Conquest," 64.

84. Tuttle, 58–59.

85. Tuttle, 58–59.

86. Tuttle, 58.

87. Tuttle, 59.

88. For more on Tuttle's discussion of Ruiz de Burton's use of this discourse of nervousness to frame her Californio subjects, men and women, in *The Squatter and the Don* as aristocratic whites, see "Symptoms of Conquest," 65–71. Tuttle also incorporates biographical information into her analysis to show that Ruiz de Burton's emphasis on Californio debilitating nervousness may be partly informed by her own experiences and that of her daughter. Tuttle concludes that "Ruiz de Burton's framing of misfortunes in terms of nervousness and disease . . . suggests that the discourse of nervousness was an important aspect of her own variegated attempts to construct herself and her fellow Californios in the terms of elite American whiteness." For the direct quotation, see "Symptoms of Conquest," 68, but for more context surrounding Ruiz de Burton's own illness related to emotional strain, see 66–68.

89. Ruiz de Burton, *Who Would Have Thought It?*, 3.

90. Alemán, "Thank God, Lolita," 96. Julie Ruiz traces Ruiz de Burton's separation of Spaniards from Native people to an earlier Anglo-American literary tradition, specifically that established by William Hickling Prescott in *The History of the Conquest of Mexico with a Preliminary View of the Ancient Mexican Civilization and the Life of Hernando Cortés* (1843) and James Fenimore Cooper in *The Prairie* (1827). See Ruiz's "Captive Identities," 117–18.

91. Ruiz de Burton, *Who Would Have Thought It?*, 30. Technically, Doña Theresa refers to them as "horrid savages" as opposed to "horrible savages, but the terms are interchangeable for her.

92. Ruiz de Burton, 27–29.

93. Ruiz de Burton, 29.

94. Ruiz de Burton, 21.

95. Alemán, "Thank God, Lolita," 103.

96. Ruiz de Burton, *Who Would Have Thought It?*, 30.

97. Alemán, "Thank God, Lolita," 103.

98. Ruiz de Burton, *Who Would Have Thought It?*, 201.

99. Ruiz de Burton, 200.

100. Ruiz de Burton, 201.

101. Ruiz de Burton, 200.

REFERENCES

Alemán, Jesse. "Citizenship Rights and Colonial Whites: The Cultural Work of María Amparo Ruiz de Burton's Novels." In *Complicating Constructions: Race, Ethnicity, and Hybridity in American Texts*, edited by David S. Goldstein and Audrey B. Thacker. Seattle: University of Washington Press, 2007.

Alemán, Jesse. "'Thank God, Lolita Is Away from Those Horrid Savages': The Politics of Whiteness in *Who Would Have Thought it?*" In *María Amparo Ruiz de Burton: Critical and Pedagogical Perspectives*, edited by Amelia María de la Luz Montes and Anne Elizabeth Goldman. New York: Palgrave, 2004.

Aranda Jr., José F. "Contradictory Impulses: María Amparo Ruiz de Burton, Resistance Theory, and the Politics of Chicano/a Studies." *American Literature* 70, no. 3 (1998): 551–79. https://www.jstor.org/stable/2902709?seq=1#metadata_info_tab_contents .

Aranda Jr., José F. 2004. "Returning California to the People: Vigilantism in *The Squatter and the Don*." In *María Amparo Ruiz de Burton: Critical and Pedagogical Perspectives*, edited by Amelia María de la Luz Montes and Anne Elizabeth Goldman. New York: Palgrave.

Dawson, Melanie V. "Ruiz de Burton's Emotional Landscape: Property and Feeling in The Squatter and the Don." *Nineteenth-Century Literature* 63, no. 1 (2008): 41–72. https://www.jstor.org/stable/10.1525/ncl.2008.63.1.41?seq=1#metadata_info_tab_contents.

DeGuzmán, María. *Spain's Long Shadow: The Black Legend, Off-Whiteness and Anglo-American Empire*. Minneapolis, MN: University of Minnesota Press, 2005.

Deines, Timothy. "Interrogating the Moral Contract in Ruiz de Burton's The Squatter and the Don." *The Yearbook of Research in English and American Literature* 22 (2006): 269–91.

De la Luz Montes, Amelia María, and Anne Elizabeth Goldman, eds. *María Amparo Ruiz de Burton: Critical and Pedagogical Perspectives*. New York: Palgrave, 2004.

Francis, Mark. *Herbert Spencer and the Invention of Modern Life*. London: Routledge Press, 2014.

Jión-King, Shimberlee. "Breaking the Silence: Contesting Manifest Destiny in María Amparo Ruiz de Burton's Who Would Have Thought It?" *Mester* 37 (2008): 19–40. https://escholarship.org/uc/item/4d77p963.

Kilcup, Karen L. 2013. "Writing Against Wilderness: María Amparo Ruiz de Burton's Elite Environmental Justice." *Western American Literature* 47 (2013): 360–85. http://muse.jhu.edu/article/500736.

Morán Gonzalez, John. *The Troubled Union: Expansionist Imperatives in Post-Reconstruction American Novels*. Columbus: Ohio State University Press, 2010.

Muñoz, José Esteban. *Disidentifications: Queers of Color and the Performance of Politics*. Minneapolis, MN: University of Minnesota Press, 1999.

Paul, Rodman W. *The Far West and the Great Plains in Transition, 1859–1900*. 2nd ed. Norman, OK: University of Oklahoma Press, 1988.

Pitt, Leonard. *The Decline of the Californios: A Social History of the Spanish-Speaking Californias: 1846–1890*. Berkeley, CA: University of California Press, 1966.

Pérez, Vincent. *Remembering the Hacienda: History and Memory in the Mexican American Southwest*. College Station, TX: Texas A&M University Press, 2006.

Raab, Josef. "The Imagined Inter-American Community of María Amparo Ruiz de Burton." *Amerikastudien* 53 (2008): 77–95.

Ruiz, Julie, "Captive Identities: The Gendered Conquest of Mexico in *Who Would Have Thought It?*" In *María Amparo Ruiz de Burton: Critical and Pedagogical Perspectives*, edited by Amelia María de la Luz Montes and Anne Elizabeth Goldman. New York: Palgrave, 2004.

Ruiz de Burton, María Amparo. *Who Would Have Thought It?*, edited by Amelia María de la Luz Montes. New York: Penguin, 2009.

Ruiz de Burton, María Amparo. *The Squatter and the Don*. Introduction by Ana Castillo. New York: Random House, 2004.

Tuttle, Jennifer S. "The Symptoms of Conquest: Race, Class, and the Nervous Body in *The Squatter and the Don*." In *María Amparo Ruiz de Burton: Critical and Pedagogical Perspectives*, edited by Amelia María de la Luz Montes and Anne Elizabeth Goldman. New York: Palgrave, 2004.

Sánchez, Rosaura, and Beatrice Pita. Introduction to *Conflicts of Interest: The Letters of María Amparo Ruiz de Burton*, edited by Rosaura Sánchez and Beatrice Pita. Houston: Arte Público Press, 2001.

Sánchez, Rosaura, and Beatrice Pita. Introduction to *The Squatter and the Don*, edited by Rosaura Sánchez and Beatrice Pita. Houston: Arte Público Press, 1995.

Warford, Elisa. "'An Eloquent and Impassioned Plea': The Rhetoric of Ruiz de Burton's The Squatter and the Don." *Western American Literature* 44 (2009): 5–21. http://muse.jhu.edu/article/266854.

Chapter Six

Violence and the Black Female Body

Deconstructing Images of Rape
in Toni Morrison's Beloved

Patricia Hopkins

In *Reconstructing Womanhood: The Emergence of the Afro-American Woman Novelist,* Hazel Carby claims, "The institutionalized rape of black women has never been as powerful a symbol of black oppression as the spectacle of lynching."[1] Likewise, in *Hine Sight,* historian Darlene Clark Hine suggests that one "of the most remarked upon but least analyzed themes in the history of southern black women deals with black women's sexual vulnerability and powerlessness as victims of rape and domestic violence."[2] The reason for this may be that when sexual exploitation is discussed, the images of the virtuous white female victim or the tortured lynched black male body overshadow that of the black female body in discourse, concerning violence and the body, which gives voice to cultural theorist Sabine Sielke's assertions in *Reading Rape,* that there are still silences in regards to this issue: "Postmodern fiction also recognizes that now that rape can be spoken, its cultural significance and function are being equivocated and displaced in turn. And while old silences may have been broken, new ones have taken shape in their stead."[3] Sielke is quite right; there are still silences that need to be broken in regards to this issue, which predates the #MeToo generation. For example, although historian Catherine Clinton echoes political activists Angela Y. Davis' statistics concerning intraracial rape,[4] which indicates that "over 90 percent of all rapes are intraracial rather than interracial."[5] Clinton, Davis, and others use these statistics to uphold the black male rapist as nothing more than myth—as they consistently use their stats to prove that black men are *not* raping white women. Consequently the gaze falls on the "myth of the black male rapist" and nothing more—here, the black female body is used as merely evidence, while at the same time she is rendered invisible; for this statistic is not so much about black women being raped as it is about black men *not* raping white women, which makes it more powerful, for the image of the violated black female body is virtually omitted. As feminist Susan Brownmiller contends in her controversially, yet groundbreaking text, *Against Our Will*, "White-on-white rape was merely 'criminal' and . . . Black-on-black rape was ignored."[6] What about a #MeToo agenda here or even an assertion that black *female* lives matter too? By keeping images of violence and rape in the period of American slavery and its aftermath, where rape is defined by southern white men as a crime committed by black men against white women,"[7] the violated black female body is rendered silent and her violation inconsequential. Toni Morrison, however, is able to ignore the statistical anomaly concerning intraracial rape in her fictional text *Beloved* and focus solely on interracial rape. Further, Morrison is able to explore images of violence done to the black female body through various images of rape without challenging the image of the black rapist as more than myth. "No single event ticks off America's political schizophrenia with greater certainty than the case of a black man accused of raping a white woman."[8] The fear of the black male as rapist still haunts and silences us.

Remember for southern whites rape meant the violation, whether real or imagined, of white female virtue by black men. Thus, Sielke insightfully points out that the sexually victimized black woman falls outside the tragic rape trope. "These texts[9] cast both white and black femininity in terms of property relations and physical violation. The crucial difference is that only black womanhood seems immune to such violation. Her injuries become negligible, and her rape finds no retribution."[10] To add salt to the wound, not only is the violated black female body not acknowledged beyond the fact that she falls outside of the trope of the tragic rape story—thus, her injuries become negligible, but, add to that her rape finds no retribution.

The image of the violated black female body is nearly rendered invisible for lack of retribution—for it is the violated black male body's injury that overshadows it. So when *Beloved*'s protagonist Sethe finds out that her husband, Halle, witnessed her violation and did nothing, she is outraged. "He saw them boys do that to me and let them keep on breathing air? He saw? He saw? He saw?"[11] It does not matter that her husband is enslaved, here you have a woman, a *wife*, who wants the man in her life, her *husband*, to come to her rescue—no different than her white female counterparts. Yet, Sethe's violation is not avenged, which Hartman classifies as "unredressed injury." "Black femaleness, as [Saidiya] Hartman puts it, is engendered 'as a condition of unredressed injury.'"[12] In fact her violation is also overshadowed by Halle's madness, again, an example of the black male body usurping the violated black female body. Still further, in the character, Stamp Paid, who ferries Sethe onto free soil, Morrison gives another glimpse of the black male perspective, which concerns the issue of the black male protecting the violated black female body: Stamp Paid was "Born Joshua, he renamed himself when he handed over his wife, Vashti, to his master's son. Handed her over in the sense that he did not kill anybody, thereby himself."[13] Again, Stamp Paid uses the image of the violated black female body as evidence—evidence of the extent of black male suffering. Vashti's violated body is just evidence and once again the black male body overshadows the victimized black female body. The characters of Sethe and Vashti, nevertheless, call for the deconstruction of the tragic story of rape, which renders the black female body as mere evidence—and her violated body not worthy to be protected or avenged.

Unlike their white female counterparts, black women, according to Morrison's text, cannot wait to be rescued or avenged. They must save themselves. First, Sethe gets her children and herself onto free soil without the aid of her husband, Halle, or any of the other men who were part of the escape plan. "I did it. I got us all out. Without Halle too. Up till then it was the only thing I ever did on my own. Decided. And it came off right, like it was supposed to. We was here. Each and every one of my babies and me too. I birthed them and I got em out and it wasn't no accident. I did that."[14] There was no knight in shining armor to rescue Sethe, no male rescuer anyway. What is important here is that Sethe, though victimized by the system is no victim. Thus, when Paul D, former slave from the Sweet Home plantation, asked Sethe why she did not run when she saw Schoolteacher come for her, she responds: "I got a tree on my back and a haint in my house, and nothing in between but the daughter I am holding in my arms. No more running—from nothing. I will never run from another thing on this earth. I took one journey and I paid for the ticket, but let me tell you something, Paul D Garner: it cost too much! Do you hear me? It cost too much."[15] Although she does not do anything as dramatic as changing her name, like Stamp Paid, Sethe realizes that she too has paid a price—and that price was too high. The American legal system, the local governing powers, the law embodied in white men, all said that Sethe was chattel and as property must be returned to those who owned her—and no man, can protect her: "when the schoolteacher found us and came busting in here with the law and a shotgun. . . . Oh, no. I wasn't going back there. I don't care who found who. Any life but not that one."[16] For Sethe, the plight of the enslaved female was something that maybe even enslaved men, like Halle, Paul D, and Stamp Paid, could not understand. "Feel how it feels to have a bed to sleep in and somebody there not worrying you to death about what you got to do each day to deserve it. Feel how that feels . . . feel how it feels to be a colored woman roaming the roads with anything God made liable to jump on you. Feel that."[17] So even though Sethe has been violated, then whipped, all while being six months pregnant, she runs alone. Sethe contends that her maternal instincts kept her going: she had a child in her womb that could not live if she died and a child across the river that would not live if she died, for only she had her milk. Thus, Sethe contends: "What I had to get through later I got through because of you [her child]. Passed right by those boys hanging in the trees . . . I walked right on by because only me had your milk, and God do what He would, I was going to get it to you."[18] Is this merely another example of the martyrdom associated with motherhood or is Morrison suggesting something more? Morrison, having Sethe pass by the lynched black male bodies, speaks volumes. The image of the lynched black male body has historically been equated to rape, the rape of the white female body. After all, it has been said that lynching is only used for one crime—that of rape. Of course, that staunch remark is only used when the raped is a white female. So Morrison having Sethe pass by those lynched men suggests that she will no longer allow the tortured lynched black male body to overshadow that of the black female body in discourse concerning violence and the body.

While the enslaved female population is still held to the same nineteen-century moral code, which the Cult-of-True-Womanhood evokes, as evidenced by Baby Suggs' comment to her granddaughter, Denver: "Grandma Baby said people look down on her because she had eight children with different men. Coloredpeople and whitepeople both look down on her for that."[19] Enslaved or free, nineteenth-century female moral code dictates that a woman must remain pure until marriage—the black female body was not excluded, enslaved or free. Thus, the nineteen-century moral code, which dictates that a man must be the protector of the female body—in some cases even from herself, does not exclude the black male body, enslaved or free. Consequently, Sethe's decree to Paul D, "They took my milk and he [Halle] saw it and didn't come down?"[20] She is speaking about her husband not protecting her body from being violated, just bearing witness to it. Yet, Morrison in no way is saying that black men are unable to protect the violated black female body. Paul D astutely says for "years [he] believed schoolteacher broke into children what Garner had raised into men."[21] If it were not for the peculiar institution black men would step up and protect their women with the same passion as their white counterparts. Besides the cultural dynamics, which leaves the violated black female body unprotected, just as schoolteacher broke men into children during American slavery, American racism would continue the job.[22] Nevertheless black men, no different than their white male counterparts, need to be needed by their women. Baby Suggs says of black men: "They encouraged you to put some of your weight in their hands,"[23] but then cannot handle all the tribulation and scars. The system renders black men responsible for black women and powerless to keep her safe at the same time. So it is not surprising that Paul D is a little annoyed when he hears that Sethe got herself and three children out without the help of any of the Sweet Home men. Morrison makes it clear; however, it is the system that fails black women, not black men. Consequently, Paul D's response after hearing how Sethe escaped: "He was proud of her and annoyed by her. Proud she had done it; annoyed that she had not needed Halle or him in the doing,"[24] is more of a reflection of the power black women are forced to cultivate and less a critique of the fact that black men did not come to the rescue of victimized black women. Just to be sure that we are not throwing the baby out with the bathwater, Morrison writes, "'while a man was nothing but a man. . . . But a son? Well now, that's somebody.'"[25] Here, Baby Suggs is talking about her son Halle. I contend this is also a dictate to the next generation—a sign of hope.

It is clear that this system of slavery and racism does not only negatively affect black men, as we study the character of Schoolteacher. Schoolteacher enters the story line when Mrs. Garner calls him to come and help her on Sweet Home after the death of her husband. "That made her feel good that her husband's sister's husband had book learning and was willing to come farm Sweet Home after Mr. Garner passed."[26] In some ways, Schoolteacher is her knight-in-shining armor—coming to her rescue and aid. This white man who would come so Mrs. Garner would not be "the only white person on the farm and a woman too."[27] He, however, was not the knight-in-shining armor foretold in fairytales. This white man did not come to rescue but to violate, corrupt, and murder. Not only are his negative actions impacted upon the enslaved of Sweet Home, Mrs. Garner is also affected—and as a white woman, she has no power to stop him. The powerlessness of Sethe and Mrs. Garner, coupled with Halle slam in the face of white male power and privilege in the embodiment of Schoolteacher. Again, this is more a commentary on the system and not against white manhood. In some ways, white women of status were more powerless than the enslaved, for they could not leave their home—they could not run. After all Sethe leaves both Mrs. Garner and Halle behind and flees. Mrs. Garner's response to Schoolteacher's action is to weep, and Halle's is to butter his face. Sethe's response, however, is to run—to save herself, thus, protecting the black female body and challenging the image of the violated female. With the traditional literary responses to sexual violation being that of death or madness, Morrison creates in literature what is reflexed by the black female community: a violated black woman who does not die or go mad; she survives.

Morrison's text not only challenges the image of the violated black female—it also challenges the traditional definition of rape. The sexual violation of Toni Morrison's protagonist, Sethe, and her sexual violation by Schooteacher's nephews, calls for the deconstruction of the term rape as well as a closer look at the sexually violated black female body within discourse on the violated body. Morrison, beginning her story in American slavery and ending it in the period of Reconstruction, focuses on the exploitation of the black female body by looking at the psychological, sexual, and physical terrorization of black female characters through generations (first, mothers, then, their daughters) by the enslaving society. It astutely shows the scars that bound these women even after their shackles had been removed. Morrison's *Beloved* is important; therefore, for it not only explores the sexual abuse of enslaved black women, with characters like Sethe, Sethe's mother, Nan—who cared for Sethe when she was a baby, Vashti—Stamp Paid's wife, and Ella—who drove Sethe's children to freedom, but moreover, challenges the rigid definition of the sexually violated body, as well as illustrating its long term effect on the mind and family—and to that end, the violated black female body is added to the discourse on violence and the body.

For Morrison, the black female body would no longer remain a silent and blind victim of rape; overshadowed by the iconic victimized black male body and violated white female body. And although this is after the text's time, I can clearly envision Morrison's fictional protagonist, Sethe, saying, in response to her violation.

Not all the sexual violations within *Beloved* are replicated in the traditional sense, as in the case of Sethe. In the case of Sethe, a nursing, expectant mother, who finds herself—due to the death of her moral slavemaster and the powerlessness of her bedridden slavemistress—in the hands of the devil, who she calls Schoolteacher. So, even though she is still nursing a crawling baby and obviously pregnant with her next, being six months along, she is forcibly held down by Schoolteacher's nephews, "those boys came in there and took my milk. That's what they came in there for. Held me down and took it."[28] Here Morrison is not only clearly describing a sexual violation, but she has also reversed penetration: Sethe's breasts are doing the penetrating and the site of this penetration is a male's orifice. Sethe's breasts become the phallic symbol, the nephews' mouths becomes the receptacle for that phallus. Sethe's breasts were swollen with milk. "I had milk . . . I was pregnant [six months] with Denver [daughter she gave birth to, by the river, the day after her escape] but I had milk for my baby girl [Beloved]. I hadn't stopped nursing her when I sent her on ahead [the escape plan from Sweet Home Plantation, called for Sethe to send her three young children along first]."[29] Breasts that are filled with milk are not only swollen, they are also hard and painful—which is similar to how an erect penis is described.

Now, instead of the hard, swollen penis forcefully penetrating the vaginal orifice, which is the classic rape, Morrison has the oral orifice, mouth, forcing itself onto a hard, swollen breast. Instead of the penis's ejaculation of its creamy-white semen, which can symbolize new life, Sethe's breasts expel their creamy-white milk, which can suggest the death of her nursing daughter, Beloved. Sethe contends, "I had to get my milk to my baby girl. Nobody was going to nurse her like me. [N]obdoy was going to get to her fast enough, or take it away when she had enough and didn't know it . . . Nobody had her milk but me."[30] To Sethe, then, her nursing daughter would die without *her* milk. Sethe was "trying to get to her children, one of whom is starving for the food she carried."[31] Sethe's milk represents life for Beloved, without that life sustaining milk; Beloved's life appears more precarious.

Instead of the traditional epoch of rape where the rapist, male, leaves inside his female victim a part of himself in the form of semen—which now through DNA testing can be as telling as leaving his fingerprint inside her womb—Morrison creates a rape whereby the victim leaves behind a part of herself in the rapists, that is, her milk. The milk-faced nephews of School-teacher are as indicative of this crime as the semen stained clothes of the traditional rape victim. "There is also my [Sethe's] husband [Halle] squatting by the churn smearing the butter as well as its clabber all over his face because the milk they took is on his mind. And as far as he is concerned, the whole world may as well know it."[32] Halle's buttered, smeared face is, as Paul D suggests, a sign that watching the sexual victimization of his wife "broke him."[33] I suggest, moreover, that it is the glaring evidence that although Sethe's sexual assault went unpunished, it did not go unseen.

The traditional rape also hints at the planting, in some cases, of seed into the victim by her rapist. The nephews achieve this fate, after the sexual assault, by using a cowhide on Sethe after she tells her Mistress about her sexual assault. They cultivate, or furrow the skin on Sethe's back with cow-hide, and then they plant the seed of a tree on her back. "Them boys found out I told on em. Schoolteacher made one open up my back, and when it closed it made a tree. It grows there still."[34] Morrison does not create the traditional rape victim who is left with life growing in her womb, in Sethe. Instead Morrison creates a non-traditional rape victim who is left with life growing on her back. On Sethe's back a tree is brought to life and is the visible evidence, which bears witness to the sexual crime—the tree on Sethe's back, the chokeberry tree in full bloom. And like Sethe's mother, who had no feeling for the seeds planted in her womb as a result of her rape by the Slaver's crew during her transatlantic passage.[35] Sethe has no feeling, literally, for the tree growing on her back, planted under the order of School-teacher by his nephews. Morrison explores this "no feelings" after a rape in another character, Sethe's mother. According to Nan, the woman who raised Sethe, Sethe's mother was "taken up many times by the crew. 'She threw them [the babies] all away but you. The one from the crew she threw away on the island. The others from more whites she also threw away. Without names, she threw them.'"[36] Sethe's mother has no feelings for these off-spring planted in her womb, a result of rape, although they are a part of her. And Sethe cannot feel anything for the tree planted on her back, although it is a part of her, because "her back skin had been dead for years."[37]

Besides giving her a non-traditional rape story, Morrison creates in Sethe the voice of resistance. In exploring the role that silence plays in perpetuating the crime of rape for generations, Sethe first resists by not remaining silent. Sethe, in telling her slave mistress, challenges the "bit"[38] placed in the mouths of victims of sexual assault, the very thing that causes them to remain silent about the crime committed against their bodies. Sethe's mother had "the bit so many times she smiled. When she wasn't smiling she smiled."[39] Sethe, then, resists by running. History is replete with accounts of the continual abuse of enslaved women by those who have the power to enslave them, therefore it is only prudent to say that the sexual exploitation of Sethe would have continued had she remained. After all, sexual violence was visited upon both her and her mother, as well as countless others with no sign of stopping. To this end, Sethe frees her daughters from suffering the same fate. Consequently, Sethe's resistance lay in breaking the cycle so that her daughters would not also suffer the same sexual abuse—and by extension, her daughters' daughters' daughters. Although many felt that Sethe was wrong for taking such drastic actions, her response is: "It's my job to know what *is* [emphasis mine] and to keep them away from what I know is terrible."[40] Sethe, in keeping her girls from having Schoolteacher measure their behinds before tearing them up,[41] stops her abuse from being reconfigured on her daughters, even if that means killing one and emotionally scaring the other.

Sethe's resistance to having the cycle of sexual violation perpetrated on her daughters, however, places her outside of the Black community. Sethe decrees that "the community step[ped] back and [held] itself at a distance."[42] It is both, Sethe's strength to resist and the Black community's guilt over their generational complicity in the wake of their victimized Black women, which cause Sethe to be held at a distance. Stamp Paid, who ferried Sethe to freedom, admits his complicity in the continual sexual abuse of his enslaved wife, Vashti; nevertheless, he still judges Sethe. Paid does not abide by Sethe's choice to kill her children, that is why he gives the newspaper clipping heralding her "crime" to Paul D.[43] Stamp Paid wanted Paul D to see that "[t]his here Sethe talked about safety with a handsaw."[44] Stamp Paid acknowledges that he is both victim and participant in the sexual exploitation of his wife, Vashti. I say victim because as an enslaved himself, he first has no legal ties to his wife, as slave marriages are not recognized, and second, he has no legal rights to speak against any White man. African Americanist, Saidiya Hartman[45] cites a good case for this: "In *Alfred v. State*, Alfred, a slave, was indicted for the murder of his overseer, Coleman . . . Alfred's action was motivated by the rape of his wife."[46] Hartman astutely surmises that "the repression of rape, the negation of kinship, and the legal invalidation of slave marriage—act in concert."[47] Like Alfred, Stamp Paid's marriage would have only been recognized in the sense that it is legally invalid, and without male kinship to speak for her, Vashti's rape would have been repressed and re-addressed as adultery, on her part, not her slavemaster's son. Alfred "was sentenced to death by hanging."[48] Vashti does not want Stamp Paid to die.

Vashti asks Stamp Paid to be complicit in the silence around her sexual violation at the hands of her slavemaster's son. Stamp Paid says, "Born Joshua, [I] renamed [myself] when [I] handed over [my] wife to [my] slave-master's son. Handed her over in the sense that [I] did not kill anybody, thereby [myself]."[49] Vashti's insistence for Stamp Paid's cooperation lay in the fact that "he [Paid to] stay alive. Otherwise, she reasoned, where and to whom could she return when the boy was through?"[50] What is Morrison suggesting by positing Sethe's violent refusal to be sexually violated with Vashti's almost complacent ideology that if all parties cooperate, when the sexual violation is over she gets to go home?

Sethe, however, is no Vashti. As stated earlier, Sethe is enraged when she finds out that her husband witnessed her sexual violation: "He saw them boys do that to me and let them keep on breathing air?"[51] Sethe's rage is strong here, and deadly. As I already suggested with the case of *Alfred v. State*, for Halle to challenge the White power structure was a suicide mission. Sethe has to know that, although Paul D reminds her of that fact.[52] All that matters is she was violated and no one came to her aid, so she is forced to rescue herself: madness or death are not options. Sethe resists further sexual attacks by absconding with her children. A year after Vashti's sexual abuse began, she "came in and sat by the window. She sat by the window looking out of it. 'I'm back,' she said. 'I'm back, Josh.'"[53] The only other thing we are told about Vashti is that she died and Stamp Paid came North without her. I think that Morrison, in positing these two characters, is suggesting that we as Black women need not "go quietly into that dark night" of sexual victimiza-tion. Maybe it is that silent, complacent surrender, which not only gave birth to the image of the "unrapeable" Black woman but allowed it to haunt the literary paradigm well into the twentieth-century.

In Sethe, Morrison has created a Black, female character who some might argue, loves too thick.[54] This rageful love causes Sethe practically to decapi-tate her "crawling-already" baby, Beloved—"littler nigger-girl eyes staring between the wet fingers that held her face so her head wouldn't fall off."[55] Is Morrison promoting infanticide? Absolutely not! What then is suggested by Sethe's actions? When it is suggested that whatever plan Sethe had when she entered that barn with her children, eighteen years ago, "didn't work."[56] Sethe counters that her plan for her children did work, because "[t]hey ain't at Sweet Home. [And] schoolteacher ain't got em."[57] Maybe Morrison is suggesting here that in order to break the cycle of generational sexual abuse one must challenge its hold, not only on oneself but the succeeding genera-tions. Sethe challenges this paradigm when she flees, as well as when she "split to the woodshed to kill her children."[58] Can Sethe's actions be consid-ered abuse as well as murder? Does Morrison suggest that Sethe is taking her children from one sort of abuse to a lesser, if you will, degree of abuse? Some suggest that Sethe is exchanging, for her children, one form of abuse— by the hands of the enslavers—for another form of abuse—by the hands of the mother. Sethe, in an almost godlike way, decreed that she would now take the life she had created—much like the biblical story of "Noah's Flood," where God takes back most of what He has created. Sethe just "[c]ollected every bit of life she had made . . . dragged them through the veil, out, away, over there where no one could hurt them."[59] Maybe it is this very godlike stance that creates this tear which causes 124 Bluestone Road to be ripped from the safety of that microcosm that is the Black community.

What is suggested by characters like: Baby Suggs, Stamp Paid, and the rest of the Black Cincinnati community, which held "itself at a distance" from Sethe,[60] is that the community does not applaud, or in some cases, even understand, much less forgive, her for sacrificing her children? For the loss of the Black community; for sending her mother-in-law, Baby Suggs to bed—slavery had knocked her down, but never kept Baby Suggs down; for the loss of her two sons, who were chased away from 124 by an angry ghost; for the death of her daughter, Beloved and the remains of the "slow-witted daughter" whom she is left to raise; Sethe says the price she paid to keep her children safe was too much. "I took one journey and paid for the ticket . . . it cost too much! Do you hear me? It cost too much."[61] Sethe laments that the price she paid to break the cycle of sexual abuse from visiting its malignant self upon her children was too high.[62] What then is a mother to do? What then is a woman to do?

This is why Morrison's *Beloved* is apropos for exploring violence and the black body in literature. In redefining the various images of rapes within the text, as well as the eventual lynching of Sethe's mother, Morrison adds images of the violated black female body to the conversation around violence and body. What is important is that #MeToo and black female lives matter, might be trendy now; however, from American slavery to the present, in both fiction and nonfiction, black female writers have been saying this all along. So maybe it should really be #YouToo, for black women have been telling the story of their sexual exploration for centuries. To read a book written by a black woman is to bear witness to the violence and sexual exploitation committed against the black body.

NOTES

1. See Hazel Carby, *Reconstructing Womanhood: The Emergence of the Afro-American Woman Novelist* (New York: Oxford University Press, 1987).

2. Darlene Clarke Hine, *Hine Sight: Black Women and the Re-Construction of American History* (New York: Carlson Publishing, 1994), 37.

3. Sabine Sielke, *Reading Rape: The Rhetoric of Sexual Violence in American Literature and Culture, 1790–1990* (Princeton, NJ: Princeton University Press, 2002), 10.

4. See Catherine Clinton, "'With a Whip in His Hand': Rape, Memory, and African-American Women," in *History and Memory in African-American Culture*. Eds. Geneviève Fabre and Robert O'Meally (New York: Oxford University Press, 1994), 205–18.

5. Angela Davis, *Women, Culture, and Politics* (New York: Vintage Books, 1990), 43.

6. Susan Brownmiller, *Against Our Will: Men, Women and Rape* (New York: Bantam, 1975), 231.

7. Crystal N. Feimster, *Southern Horrors: Women and the Politics of Rape and Lynching* (Cambridge: Harvard University Press, 2009), 5.

8. Brownmiller, *Against Our Will*, 230.

9. Sielke here is referring to Elizabeth Keckley, *Behind the Scenes. Or, Thirty Years as a Slave, and Four Years in the White House* (New York: Oxford University Press, 1988); and Ann Petry, *The Street*. 1946. Reprint. (Boston: Houghton, 1974). Sielke's comments can also apply to Harriet Jacobs, *Incidents in the Life of a Slave Girl: Written by Herself* (Cambridge: Harvard University Press, 1987); Noni Carter, *Good Fortune* (New York: Simon and Schuster, 2010); and Nnedi Okorafor, *Who Fears Death* (New York: Daw, 2014).

10. Sielke, *Reading Rape*, 27.

11. Toni Morrison, *Beloved* (New York: Plume, 1987), 69.

12. Sielke, *Reading Rape*, 27.

13. Morrison, *Beloved*, 184.

14. Morrison, 162.

15. Morrison, 15.

16. Morrison, 42.

17. Morrison, 67–68.

18. Morrison, 198.

19. Morrison, 209.

20. Morrison, 69.

21. Morrison, 220.

22. Carter G. Woodson, *The Mis-Education of the Negro* (Independent Publishing, 1933), 55. Here I refer to Carter G. Woodson and the lasting, generational effects of racism—"If you can control a man's thinking, you do not have to worry about his action. When you determine what a man shall think you do not have to concern yourself about what he will do. If you make a man feel that he is inferior, you do not have to compel him to accept an inferior status, for he will seek it himself. If you make a man think that he is justly an outcast, you do not have to order him to the back door. He will go without being told; and if there is no back door, his very nature will demand one."

23. Morrison, *Beloved*, 22.

24. Morrison, 8.

25. Morrison, 22–23.

26. Morrison, 36.

27. Morrison, 37.

28. Morrison, 16.

29. Morrison, 16.

30. Morrison, 16.

31. Morrison, 31.

32. Morrison, 70.

33. Morrison, 69.

34. Morrison, 17.

35. Morrison, 62.

36. Morrison, 62.
37. Morrison, 18.
38. Morrison, 69. Here I use "bit" like Paul D when he tells Sethe he could not speak to Halle, when Halle had his face covered with butter, because he "had a bit in [his] mouth." Bit has two meaning here, a physical metal implement which forces the mouth to remain open damaging the corners of the mouth, and the metaphorical "bit" of slavery, which stops the mouth from telling the horrors of such a "peculiar institution."
39. Morrison, 203.
40. Morrison, 165.
41. Morrison, 203.
42. Morrison, 177.
43. Morrison, 154.
44. Morrison, 164.
45. Saidiya Hartman, *Scenes of Subjection: Terror, Slavery, and Self-Making in Nineteenth-Century America* (New York: Oxford Univeristy Press, 1997).
46. Hartman, 84.
47. Hartman, 84.
48. Hartman, 84.
49. Morrison, *Beloved*, 184-85. The irony here is in the name "Stamp Paid." Stamp Paid feels that by turning away and not "seeing," "challenging" the sexual exploitation of Vashti, he is no longer indebted for anything, in ferrying runaways across the Ohio River. It is Vashti who is raped for a year. I agree, as her husband, a crime is also committed against him, but, "Stamp Paid," to me signals an invisible Vashti. Paid's violation, as the husband, appears to supersede the violation of the victim, his wife. Paid reasons that "[w]ith that gift [handing his wife over], he didn't owe anybody anything. Whatever his obligations were, that act [handing his wife over] paid them off."
50. Morrison, 185.
51. Morrison, 69.
52. Morrison, 69.
53. Morrison, 233.
54. Morrison, 164.
55. Morrison, 150.
56. Morrison, 164.
57. Morrison, 165.
58. Morrison, 158.
59. Morrison, 163.
60. Morrison, 177.
61. Morrison, 15.
62. Morrison, 107–8. Since Morrison does address the Black male prisoners forced to perform oral sex on the prison guards, sexual exploitation, used here is not gender specific. "Kneeling in the mist they waited for the whim of a guard, or two, or three. Or maybe all of them wanted it. Wanted it from one prisoner in particular or none—or all. . . . Occasionally a kneeling man chose gunshot in his head as the price, maybe, of taking a bit of foreskin with him to Jesus."

REFERENCES

Brownmiller, Susan. *Against Our Will: Men, Women and Rape*. New York: Bantam, 1975.
Carby, Hazel. *Reconstructing Womanhood: The Emergence of the Afro-American Woman Novelist*. New York: Oxford University Press, 1987.
Clinton, Catherine. "'With a Whip in His Hand': Rape, Memory, and African-American Women," in *History and Memory in African-American Culture*. Eds. Geneviève Fabre and Robert O'Meally. New York: Oxford University Press, 1994.
Davis, Angela. *Women, Culture, and Politics*. New York: Vintage Books, 1990.

Feimster, Crystal N. *Southern Horrors: Women and the Politics of Rape and Lynching.* Cambridge: Harvard University Press, 2009.

Hartman, Saidiya. *Scenes of Subjection: Terror, Slavery, and Self-Making in Nineteenth-Century America.* New York: Oxford University Press, 1997.

Hine, Darlene Clarke. *Hine Sight: Black Women and the Re-Construction of American History.* New York: Carlson Publishing, 1994.

Morrison, Toni. *Beloved.* New York: Plume, 1987.

Sielke, Sabine. *Reading Rape: The Rhetoric of Sexual Violence in American Literature and Culture, 1790–1990.* Princeton: Princeton University Press, 2002.

Woodson, Carter G. *The Mis-Education of the Negro.* Independent Publishing, 1933.

Chapter Seven

Resist, Survive, Endure

Empowered Female Characters in Patrick O'Brian's Aubrey/Maturin Novels

James Cornette

Responding to the theme of this 2019 International Conference on the Global Status of Women and Girls, "Intersectionality: Understanding Women's Lives and Resistance in the Past and Present," I propose to demonstrate the relevance of Patrick O'Brian's Aubrey/Maturin historical novels to those key concepts of *intersectionality* and *resistance*. O'Brian's fiction provides a window into the status and treatment of women and girls in the early decades of the nineteenth century, as he frequently explores the era's slowly emerging societal consciousness of the rights of women as a vital element in the struggle against tyranny. The twenty novels in this incomparable series, from *Master and Commander* to *Blue at the Mizzen*, are framed by the Napoleonic Wars, with particular focus on their maritime aspects. In many instances O'Brian's two central characters, devoted to the cause of defeating Napoleon's tyrannical designs, confront the destructive effects of Eurocentric colonialism and exploitation of "subject people" on "the far side of the world." As a valiant Royal Navy captain and his exceptionally capable medical officer,[1] Jack Aubrey and Stephen Maturin participate in many eye-opening events that lie well beyond the ken of the "landlubbers" back home.

DIANA AND DIL

Dr. Maturin undergoes just such an eventful combination of personal experiences in India, one that was anticipated, and another that unfolded unexpectedly but nonetheless as if it were predestined for him. In the third novel of the O'Brian saga, *H.M.S. Surprise*, Stephen arrives in Bombay after enduring numerous challenges both at sea and ashore. In the crucial role of ship's surgeon aboard the vessel commanded by Post Captain Aubrey, he has been a key participant in a mission to the Malay Peninsula and the Sultan of Prabang, where a capable British ambassador has been sent to negotiate a strategically essential treaty on behalf of the Crown. The emissary, unfortunately, is a man in failing health who dies en route, despite Stephen's efforts to remedy his fatal illness, and the mission ultimately collapses. Dr. Maturin is carrying his own physical and emotional wounds as well, having been betrayed back in England by the irresistible passion of his life, Diana Villiers, one of the most mercurial and fascinating characters in O'Brian's extensive cast. Diana, daughter of an English general staff officer posted to India, had come of age as part of the Raj, and was given in marriage to her father's aide-de-camp, a young officer with excellent family connections. Sadly, his promising life was cut short in an uprising of anti-imperialist rebels. Her father having also been killed, she had returned to England with no resources but her remarkable beauty, sharp intellect, and an unrelenting determination not to be defeated by a patriarchal and often misogynistic social order.

Maturin's equally remarkable intelligence was no protection against the magnetic attraction that drew him to her, and Diana recognized in the unhandsome and rather maladroit Stephen a man whose honesty and directness were refreshing, even stimulating enough to draw her toward him as well. Yet Diana could not allow herself to forget that she might never achieve independence and success in her world without exploiting her natural advantages of grace and beauty before time robbed her of feminine leverage. Maturin, at least at this stage in his career, lacked the financial power and status to alleviate her anxieties about vulnerability, and Diana was unable to commit herself to him romantically, however much he desired that. In short, she abandoned him, becoming mistress to a wealthy and worldly, socially adept and cunning manipulator of the main chance, Richard Canning, who had preceded Maturin to India with Diana in tow.

In chapter 7 of *H.M.S. Surprise*, O'Brian contrives in a plausible fashion—and almost in the manner of a Sophoclean rendition of tragic destiny—to interweave two strands of the potent drives of Stephen's life: his consuming love for Diana and his passion for alleviating the suffering of other humans, especially those lacking the power to protect themselves from harm. When his empathetic nature is stirred by a chance encounter with an impoverished Indian child, he is at first only vaguely aware of her ironical fitness to be his *own* protector, although she senses with uncanny intuition that Stephen is himself a potential victim. The foreshadowed encounter with Diana, despite being actualized a bit later in the novel's sequence of events, thus sets the stage for Stephen's vital relationship with Dil. She is a girl of about ten years of age, who lives largely by her wits in the densely populated city of

Bombay—a charming urchin, if you will, somewhat reminiscent of Charles Dickens' "Artful Dodger," Jack Dawkins, in *Oliver Twist*. At the time of their meeting Maturin has been attempting to recover his sense of emotional balance by wandering Bombay's streets, dressed in Indian fashion, an emaciated and unremarkable Englishman. In truth he is the bastard son of an Irish soldier and a Catalonian mother, whose months at sea have left him with a leathery, tanned countenance and the ability to take in all that the great city can reveal to his inquiring eye without arousing so much as a casual curiosity about the insatiable observer.

Dil, however, has an even keener eye, and takes note of him. Indeed, their lives first intersect when she rescues him from being trampled by a herd of Indian buffalo in a city square, grasping the sleeve of his garment and pulling him to safety. From that moment she adopts him as if he were her ward, conversing with him in Urdu, a language of which he has previously acquired some knowledge from Asian members of *Surprise*'s crew. In a charming reversal of age-appropriate roles, Stephen the accomplished physician and surgeon, multi-lingual natural philosopher, expert and intrepid intelligence agent for the British government, becomes her devoted pupil. He describes her in his vividly detailed journal as follows: "This dear child Dil teaches me a great deal, talking indefatigably, a steady flow of comment and narrative, with incessant repetition where I do not understand—she insists on being understood, and no evasion deceives her," for she is a bright and ". . . fearless creature that looks me directly in the face as though I were a not very intelligent tame animal, . . . as though I, too were a child." In the same passage Stephen goes on to describe Dil's yearning for a "silver bangle," which most of the Indian children seem to be "encumbered with, and clank as they go." He expresses his wish to save her from "the gutters and bazaars of Bombay," being tempted to buy her from her ancient guardian, a crone who has already offered her for sale as a marketable, guaranteed virgin. However, he recognizes that his desire to be her protector may be delusional. In less than a year, Stephen foresees, Dil will be living in a brothel, but he wonders if placing her in a European household would be preferable: "A servant, washed and confined? Could I keep her [safe]? For how long? Endow her? It is hard to think of her lively young spirit sinking, vanishing in the common lot. I shall advise with Diana: I have a groping notion of some unidentified common quality [they share]."[2]

Stephen introduces the two of them after a chance—or fated?—meeting in the teeming streets of Bombay, and Diana greets Stephen with unfeigned delight while also taking to Dil with gracious and genuine affection at first sight. Dil, however, regards Diana with suspicion, and despite a willingness to accompany Stephen as a guest in the woman's home, never fully accepts Diana's blandishments without guarded reluctance. It is clear that Dil sees her as a rival for Stephen's attention, but also that the child understands his vulnerability and wants to draw him back from the danger that Diana represents. Undeterred, however, Stephen shortly falls even more fully under Diana's seemingly gravitational dominion—and it is noteworthy that O'Brian at various times subtly associates her with the power of the moon and moonlight throughout a lengthy sequence of novels; yet she is a much more individuated character, complex and down-to-earth, than a merely allegorical representation of Diana the moon goddess. Stephen is buoyed up by her expressions of welcoming affection and her recognition of the virtue in Stephen's desire to rescue Dil, as well as by her willingness to support his efforts to do so, and he sets out to provide a gift for the child that he is certain Dil will receive with gladness. He purchases a set of the silver bracelets she longs for, and the gifting scene is one of the most touching moments in the novel, particularly so with respect to O'Brian's characteristic avoidance of anything that smacks of maudlin sentimentality:

> She put one on and another; and the rapture of possession seized her. She burst into wild laughter, slipped them all on, all off, all on in a different order, patting them, talking to them, giving them each a name. She leapt up and spun, jerking her thin arms to make the bracelets clink. . . . She ran skipping down the hill: he watched her until she vanished in the twilight, her gleaming arms held out like wings. . . .[3]

When Stephen returns to visit with Diana once again, he summons up courage enough to propose marriage, an offering of self undoubtedly given wings by Dil's joyous response to his gift, and by the angelic image still present in his mind. Diana is amazed by the proposal, recognizing that he not only loves her but intends to save her from an ignominious situation. Diana is deeply moved, even astonished, telling him that his words are the most valuable gift she has ever been offered. She asks for time to consider the proposal, and promises him an answer in Calcutta, the city to which she and Canning will shortly be traveling on his official business, because she knows the *Surprise's* mission will take the ship there as well. Even in the face of his intense disappointment, Maturin clings to the hope that Calcutta will bring the fulfillment of his wishes. However, in short order the narrative's trajectory shifts dramatically, although again exhibiting O'Brian's penchant for revealing the most intense occurrences in the lives of his characters through spare, plain description, and a Sophoclean starkness. When Dr. Maturin receives notice from a shipmate that Aubrey has called all hands to report on board *Surprise* immediately and is in a "hellfire hurry" to be at sea, he sets off for the docks himself and passes by the street on which Dil lives with her elderly guardian—only to see the crone standing over Dil's enshrouded body, protesting that she cannot afford the cost of ritual cremation. The child, whom he had watched as she danced away with her new bracelets jingling the music of her delight, is now, in startling suddenness, a lifeless form on the dusty street.

One of the people gathered at the scene protests that the little girl cannot be given the proper ceremonial rites. "Here is no one of her caste," declares an onlooker, and the murmurs of woeful assent are heard. "But with a famine coming, no man dared look beyond the caste he belonged to. 'I am of her caste,' [says] Stephen to the man in front of him, touching his shoulder. 'Tell the woman I will buy the child. Friend, tell the woman I will buy the child and take it down. I will attend to the fire.'" From that point onward, he assumes responsibility for Dil's last rites, and the chapter closes with a downcast Stephen seated by the immediate waterside, transfixed by the dying flames of Dil's funeral pyre. The solemn words of Catholic liturgy, Latin words from the requiem mass of Stephen's own faith, are heard issuing softly from his mouth. As O'Brian writes, "'. . . nunc et in hora mortis nostrae,' he repeated yet again, and felt the lap of water on his foot. He looked up. The people had gone; the pyre was no more than a dark patch with the sea hissing in its embers and he was alone. The tide was rising fast."[4]

This experience becomes one of the most transformative in Maturin's life, inasmuch as his efforts to save the woman he adores, Diana, both from her own willfulness and the greedy lust of a powerful rival, have almost certainly failed.[5] Worse still, his desire to rescue Dil, the extraordinary Indian child, from a cruel destiny, has been thwarted by a brutal criminal act, one in which Stephen's own loving and humane intentions had played a crucial part—since the young girl was surely murdered for her silver treasures, perhaps by one of the other children. One could be pardoned at this point for recalling the words of Oedipus as he reflects on the disastrous consequences of acts he committed with righteous intentions, only to discover that he was predestined to tragic fulfillment of a plot engineered for him by fate. He declares that Apollo has been the author of that fate, but he also acknowledges that "the hand" bringing about the predestined actions was his own. When Oedipus reveals himself after self-mutilation—having removed the eyes that had been useless to save him from delusion—he starkly accepts his role as co-author of his destiny.[6] In a similar fashion, O'Brian enmeshes his characters, and especially Dr. Maturin, in the timeless struggle of human rationality with something too systematically embedded in the fabric of reality to be called mere randomness or Accident. Driven by the genuineness of his emotional responses to the needs and hopes of others, Maturin displays his capacity to take ownership of Dil's destiny, and to recognize the rising of an eternal tide of grief for the human condition. Yet O'Brian's reader senses that Stephen will find the strength to continue applying the surgeon's and caregiver's "hand"—despite the abiding threat that a tragic, Sophoclean predestination may nevertheless defeat his best intentions.

EMILY AND SARAH

As is typically the case in the twenty-volume *roman fleuve* of the Aubrey/
Maturin series, the reader discovers the full impact of Stephen's failure to
preserve Dil's precious life only little by little, over the course of several
ensuing novels. Quite a bit further on, in fact, in the fourteenth of the series,
The Nutmeg of Consolation, O'Brian revisits the "rescue the perishing"
theme with particular emphasis on the plight of children in tragic circumstances. This novel is the second in a sequence of five involving a circumnavigation of the world. At something like the halfway point, the *Surprise*
needs to make landfall at Sweetings Island in the South Pacific to replenish
foodstuffs and water.[7] The Melanesian island is oddly quiet, although Aubrey knows that it is inhabited and has offered a welcome haven for whaling
ships in the past. When Stephen goes ashore in a small craft, accompanied by
Jack and a few crewmembers, expecting a friendly greeting from the residents, instead they discover a village that more appropriately could be called
a collection of charnel houses. The largest structure they visit contains an
astonishing number of corpses, and Dr. Maturin quickly recognizes the signs
of a devastating smallpox epidemic. He urges all who have never been
marked by the dread pox to touch nothing and return to the ship as quickly as
possible. Stephen, Jack, and one other shipmate, all of whom had survived
infection as a child, nevertheless walk inland a short distance to look for
edible fruits and a source of fresh water. They are stunned to come upon two
native children, both girls, who are very much alive. They are barely skin and
bones, obviously starving, fearful but too weakened to run and hide. It is
clear that they have miraculously survived the plague and, if they are to
continue living, must be taken off the island and cared for properly.

   Despite Captain Aubrey's understandable concern that his ship might still
become infected, he accepts Dr. Maturin's assurance that the two children
could no longer carry the lethal agency, which has otherwise eradicated the
entire island's population. He concedes that Stephen's to save them from
certain starvation is the only humane choice, and he welcomes the two girls
aboard the *Surprise*. There is little doubt that Jack feels a degree of guilty
accountability for their fate, because he has seen multiple instances where
contact with "civilized" and often predatory Europeans has been anything but
a blessing to native peoples. Captain Aubrey actually harbors an indignant
"resentment for his own unshared horror" toward those who brought the
pestilence to this island, and, under the weight of these melancholy thoughts,
sinks for a while into a sullen mood.[8] Although the rescued children are also,
at first, understandably disoriented and frightened, they are given the "Christian" names of Emily and Sarah Sweetings, and are placed under the watch-
ful eye of Jemmy Ducks, the crewman in charge of the ship's assortment of
poultry and livestock. They rather quickly become his willing, enthusiastic

assistants, and naturally continue to see Maturin as their adoptive father, clinging to him whenever danger threatens.

The irony of the "christening" of the Sweetings sisters is plainly apparent, though O'Brian does not call special attention to it. Even so, it is a feature of the enduring friendship of Aubrey and Maturin that Stephen enjoys prodding Jack about the sanctimonious and frequently hypocritical ways in which the English view the world and England's role in it. To Dr. Maturin, the Royal Navy's penchant for blowing its enemies' ships and their crews zealously "to Kingdom Come"[9] seems more heavily dependent for its justification on Old Testament theology than New. Hearing such arguments, Jack at times will grant some concessions to his learned friend's wisdom, conceding that Dr. Maturin is a "deep old file."[10] As a genuine Enlightenment *philosophe*, Stephen's comprehensive vision inclines him to make wry comments about willful human self-delusions, although, like Sophocles, he recognizes that good, bad, and indifferent forces intersect in ways beyond the control of well-meaning individuals. Despite this penchant for fatalism, however, Maturin never ceases striving to alleviate the unfortunate consequences of what might be called "tragic intersectionality."

Stephen's Melanesian episode has subjected him and several of his shipmates to what certainly could be termed a "gothic" experience. The charnelhouse encounter has its numerous counterparts in literary Gothicism during the early nineteenth century. And, as O'Brian's multi-volume novel evolves, we are frequently reminded that Dr. Maturin is often up to his elbows in blood, that he has opened skulls and sawed off limbs, and that his "natural" environment in the surgical cockpit aboard a ship engaged in thunderous battle is almost always a hellish place. Patrick O'Brian undoubtedly relished working knowledgeably within a comprehensively wide literary tradition, from classic to modern, and it is arguable that Captain Aubrey's accomplished "chirurgical" friend and shipmate was allusively a reminder of the character created by the Irish author, Charles Maturin. The most memorable fictional creation of that real-life Maturin was *Melmoth the Wanderer*, a man driven to traverse much of the known world in search of someone who will release him from the Faustian bargain he has made with the devil. In his wanderings, Melmoth, gifted with an extraordinary life span and therefore a wealth of earthly experiences, is unable to find anyone willing to take on his burden and void the satanic contract. After four volumes developing Melmoth's episodic and chill-inducing adventures, Charles Maturin propels the wanderer to his last moments with the conclusive realization that no one acquainted with the wretchedness of human experience would ever trade his or her soul for a preternaturally lengthened life on earth.[11] Although Stephen Maturin never relents in his dedication to reducing the sum total of suffering in this world, he is a bedeviled wanderer whose nights are often restless and deprived of comforting dreams, unless they are brought into existence by the

power of laudanum—the alcoholic tincture of opium. This addictive substance, one of the most often prescribed medicines in the pharmacology of
pain relief during Stephen's era,[12] becomes his own Faustian blessing and
curse over much of the Aubrey/Maturin saga. Indeed, in *The Commodore*,
seventeenth novel in the series, despite having broken the habit that had
nearly cost his life in *The Letter of Marque*,[13] he is tempted by cruelly
stressful circumstances to once again resort to its restorative and soothing
potency, rationalizing that there is an apothecary's shop nearby and "'there is
something to be said for a stupid tranquility at times.'" Nonetheless, refusing
to yield to the temptation, Dr. Maturin firmly checks himself, declaring
aloud: "'Vade retro, Satanas!'"[14]

While still dealing with the tasks undertaken in *The Nutmeg of Consolation*, however—and once the *Surprise* reaches a key objective in its voyage,
Sydney harbor in New South Wales (Australia)—Stephen endeavors to find a
proper orphanage where the girls can be provided an appropriate place to
live. He reasons that they surely could not be afforded such a home as
permanent passengers on a man-of-war. Neither could he reasonably expect
them to adjust painlessly to so-called civilized life in England. Seeking a
solution to this dilemma, he delivers them to an establishment recommended
by the governor's wife, Mrs. Macquarie. It is an orphanage vouched for by
this "good and kind" woman, though Jemmy Ducks sorely dreads leaving the
sisters there, in so godforsaken "a country as this, God love us."[15] Such
institutions typically housed illegitimate offspring of female members of the
transported population, sometimes aboriginal infants and children, and not a
few unfortunates who came into this world (or were conceived) "between
decks" on various ships making landfall in Sydney's Port Jackson. Upon
being introduced to this place of presumed sanctuary, care, feeding, and even
education, the girls are quick to assert, bluntly and aggressively, that they
have already found a true home among their family of seafaring men aboard
the Surprise, and want nothing to do with the other orphans. Indeed, these
ingenious, resistant, and determined girls almost instantly escape, find their
own way back to their ship, discard their ladylike frocks, and scramble up the
rigging into the uppermost crosstrees. It becomes transparently clear to Stephen that Sarah and Emily are going to be inconsolable if the *Surprise* is to
leave Sydney without them. Moved by their distress and determination, he
declares: "Come down, then. . . . We shall not turn you ashore,"[16] and "the
deep old file" surrenders to their greater wisdom, concluding that he will
have to take responsibility for their upbringing back in England, where he
has conscientious friends who will help to make their adaptation to European
life attainable.

Until that time arrives, he knows that their amazing facility with language
will be greatly to their advantage; they are already capable of functioning
with equal adeptness in the maritime lingo of the ship's often-bawdy crew, as

well as in the more formal speech of Dr. Maturin and the ship's officers. Therefore, once the circumnavigation is completed, the girls are taken under the wing of the good Mrs. Broad, the guiding genius of an establishment known as the Grapes, which Stephen has made his London home since the early days of his friendship with Captain Aubrey. While still in the Pacific, however, the two Sweetings show both their adaptability and intuitive intelligence on many occasions, as in the instance described in a passage occurring early in the next novel (the 15th), *The Truelove*. Having carried out a difficult and protracted, pre-dawn surgery below decks, Dr. Maturin emerges just before noon, meeting "a usual morning procession" of Jemmy Ducks carrying hencoops, Sarah bearing one of the hens, and Emily shepherding Jezebel the goat. The children bow, smile, and offer morning greetings, and "then Emily [says] in her clear child's voice 'Miss is weeping and wringing her hands, way up forward.'" At first Stephen only marvels at the gentle mastery the Sweetings sisters are exerting over the animals, thinking to himself, "'that goat is a froward goat and the speckled hen a cross ill-natured bird, yet they allow themselves to be led and carried without so much as an oath,'" and a moment passes before he can grasp "the force of her remark. 'Ay,' he [replies], shaking his head."[17]

CLARISSA

The "Miss" remarked upon by Emily is one Clarissa Harvill, a young woman who has earlier been brought onto the ship by a seaman, midshipman William Oakes, and hidden in the cable tiers below decks as a stowaway. Although, as the reader later discovers, Clarissa is a well-born English woman, she was sentenced to the penal colony at Botany Bay. She is now crying because she is certain that the ship will abandon her on Norfolk Island, along with Oakes. Largely because Maturin is puzzled how a young woman with gracious manners and obvious intelligence could have become a transported convict, he befriends her and soon learns enough to recognize that she has been the victim of injustice. He gradually persuades Aubrey that she should by rights be given the opportunity to marry Oakes (as both William and Clarissa desire), and that the *Surprise* ought to resist any efforts by a pursuing vessel to recapture her and return her to Botany Bay. Jack, being charmed by her seaman-like demeanor and willingness to endure hardship without complaint, assents to the plan, and even offers to have a bolt of scarlet silk, which he had bought in Batavia for his wife Sophia, worked up into a wedding dress for her. Regrettably, the marriage which Aubrey and Maturin enable soon proves to be vexed by "dirty weather," as British tarpaulins would put it. The ship's company begin to show either favoritism or dislike for Clarissa. Rumors of liaisons with various other men besides her husband start to reach Maturin's ears. At one point she tries to remain hidden in her cabin for several days, admitting Stephen only because he has become her physician, and he discovers signs of physical assault, even a recently blackened eye.

While the ship is in anchorage offshore of a Pacific island, she and Maturin take a botanizing walk inland, during which she confides many details of her past. He learns that Clarissa was born into a well-to-do English family and that her girlhood was beset by male sexual predators among her relatives. Having been abused from late childhood onward, and ultimately discarded because of her independent disposition, she had found employment as a bookkeeper in an upscale brothel, Mother Abbott's in St. James's,[18] where she was also expected to serve as a prostitute to some of the more refined clients of London's smart set. These biographical details are of singular interest to Maturin the physician, a surgeon whose pervading interest in human psychology is deeply engaged by her entirely mechanistic understanding of sexuality. She cannot fathom why men, even her husband, can be so impassioned and possessive about sexual encounters. (William's intense jealousy, of course, explains her bruises.) Her life experiences have left her with no capacity for erotic pleasure, and yet Stephen discovers that her mental acuity is keen, and that she does find deep satisfaction in the natural world, the sea-borne environment, the creatures of the sea, the land, and the air.

Being himself a naturalist who observes living things of all shapes and sizes with meticulous attention to the smallest details of anatomy and behavior, Dr. Maturin finds Clarissa to be the most entrancing subject of his many scientific studies. More vitally, his humane and unwavering emotional support for her finally makes possible her reconciliation with her husband—who, at the end of the novel, has redeemed himself by behaving "in a seamanlike, officerlike fashion" and by sincerely atoning for his wretched actions as a jealous cuckold. Captain Aubrey has consequently rewarded Oakes, giving him command of a captured vessel—the *Truelove*—designating him as the "prizemaster" who is to receive a significant share of credit from the admiralty after the ship undergoes inspection in Batavia. Aubrey displays open-handedness to both Oakes and his wife when he declares, "I shall [also] make an advance on your pay and prize-money to bear your charge from Batavia home"—to England.[19]

Even more crucially for Stephen, on this homeward voyage the *Surprise's* surgeon has arranged for Clarissa to act as trusted courier of a stunning revelation, intended for the chief of intelligence, Sir Joseph Blaine, at Whitehall in London. Encoded in the encrypted message is the identity of Napoleon's most dangerous spy in the British government, along with Maturin's expression of complete faith in the source of the intelligence, Clarissa herself. Although lacking Stephen's formal education in scientific observation,

Clarissa had always studied the clientele at Mother Abbott's closely—every detail of appearance and style, every behavioral quirk—and her keen recollections have given Stephen all the clues he needs to solve a mystery that had agonizingly defied untangling for most of a decade. Thus, Clarissa Oakes becomes an agency for a kind of poetic justice in a cycle of novels whose author's vision of the world, as often as not, denies his characters such a pleasing symmetry. But like many women and girls in the Aubrey/Maturin series, she is a robust individual, a phoenix rising from the ashes of defeat to gain at least a provisional, perhaps an enduring victory. Her return to England on a vessel named *Truelove* may well be more than fitting, after all.[20]

The idealization of true love is thematically important throughout the Aubrey/Maturin cycle, although scarcely within the tradition of the popular "romance novel." Patrick O'Brian perhaps came closest to embodying the female ideal of virtue, constancy, and beauty in the person of Jack Aubrey's lovely wife, Sophie (née Sophia Williams). Indeed, Stephen never ceases to be charmed by her sweet benevolence throughout the series of novels, becoming her brotherly confidant and advisor early on, while using all of his powers of persuasion and guileful manipulation to bring Jack and Sophie together and to keep their marriage intact. This is a daunting challenge for him, since she maintains an almost cloistered innocence about sexual matters, while Jack is far more inclined to fulfill the Royal Navy's contemporary maxim that every husband would become a bachelor east of Gibraltar. However, O'Brian explores the motif of the unbreakable bond of married love at length in *Treason's Harbour*, ninth novel in the series, focusing especially on a Neapolitan woman, Laura Fielding.

LAURA

Mrs. Fielding complicates the lives of both Aubrey and Maturin, and O'Brian deploys all of his ironical talents in developing her character and fashioning the elements of plot that make it difficult for either of the men to determine a clear course of action. In many respects Laura becomes the east-of-Gibraltar version of Sophie, but oddly enough, one whose devotion to her own husband has to be expressed in ways that Sophie's moralistic mother, a domineering woman who possessed an "unprincipled rectitude,"[21] could never have countenanced. Sophie Aubrey's moral sense draws from a deeper well of human kindness than that of dame Williams, but the reader understands that Jack's spouse is blessed never to have been confronted with the dilemma faced by Laura Fielding.

Like Sophie, Laura is the wife of a Royal Navy officer, but her husband, Lieutenant Charles Fielding, is a currently a prisoner of war. Prior to the opening events of *Treason's Harbour* he has been captured by the French and, after an unsuccessful attempt to escape from Verdun, is now imprisoned in the infamous facility at Bitche. These facts are unknown initially to either Jack Aubrey or Stephen Maturin. However, the two men are very much aware that Laura Fielding is a charming and singularly attractive woman, admired by all the British personnel currently on station in Malta, where she hosts musical soirées and earns a modest income by giving lessons in Italian. Jack and Stephen do not know, more crucially, that she has been compromised by one of the three French spy networks operating in Valletta, an espionage ring masterminded by the deadly André Lesueur, whose minions have persuaded Mrs. Fielding that her assistance in gaining desirable intelligence will ensure her husband's survival and perhaps even buy his freedom. Lesueur's objective is ultimately to draw both Aubrey and Maturin into his web through Fielding's coerced compliance—and, because the French spy master has also deduced that Stephen was responsible for the deaths of two of Napoleon's intelligence agents in America, Maturin's seduction is to be only a prelude to his capture, torture, and murder.

Laura has no knowledge of the sinister depths of this plotting, and she is singularly lacking in the subtle skills of a duplicitous manipulator. In fact, Stephen senses that something is amiss even before any threads of the web become visible. During the scene in which he first observes her at a public gathering of naval officers at a streetside café, he muses on the value such a woman *could* have to a spy organization—a natural mental exercise to a man who has already become a master of spycraft in his own right, and who has also been subjected to imprisonment and torture by another of the competing agencies of Napoleon's intelligence apparatus. He quietly contemplates "how well she took [those officers'] open though respectful admiration, their kindly banter and their flights of wit—no missishness, no bridling, no simpering but no bold over-confidence either." These qualities cause Maturin to watch her "with curiosity, and with something more," because her amiable and genteel cultivation of relationships among the officer corps suggests that she might have more than "gallantry or profit" in mind—perhaps "intelligence." He recognizes that he must cautiously but professionally "sift the matter," although his suspicions could well be groundless, and he persuades himself "that this [is] the right course since he [likes] her company, [likes] her musical evenings, and [is] convinced that he could govern any untimely emotion that might rise in his heart."[22]

Maturin soon discovers that Mrs. Fielding's challenge to his self-governance will be extreme. Driven by the threat that her husband's captors intend to kill the lieutenant unless she is able to compromise Stephen and deliver valuable information to the French, she invites Aubrey, Maturin, and an assortment of British officers to one of her musical gatherings. Although her performance as hostess delights most of the men present, her pianoforte playing falls well below her usual standard, and both Jack and Stephen, accomplished amateurs on violin and cello, are puzzled by her uncharacteristic awkwardness. They are also nonplussed when she makes it evident that she wishes to have Stephen linger with her after all the other guests have departed. This is mildly stunning to Aubrey, since "Lucky Jack" has earlier been tempted to make his own Italian lesson something more rambunctious, only to be gracefully and firmly rebuffed. Even so, the benevolent Jack "always esteemed women who refused him kindly."[23] Having previously rescued Mrs. Fielding's huge dog, Ponto, from drowning in a deep cistern, Jack has frequently been obliged to endure the grateful animal's public, noisy, and clumsy displays of adoration. These embarrassing episodes have already identified him in gossipy Valletta as Mrs. Fielding's not-so-secret lover, and he is being forced to accept "only the inconveniences of the situation" with none of its actual benefits.[24] The idea that Maturin should be the beneficiary of the red-haired beauty's favors adds a bit more salt to the wound.

There follows one of O'Brian's most artfully crafted, almost painfully comic scenes, in which Laura attempts a seduction that she clearly has no inclination to accomplish, and Stephen struggles mightily to restrain his own carnal impulses while trying to assess the larger "situation" with objective rationality. Ultimately Laura's impossible mission fails because her devotion to Charles will not allow her to consummate it, and also because Stephen proves yet again to be "a deep old file": "It is clear that you wish me to do something of a particular nature," he says to her. "For a woman of your kind to propose such a sacrifice it must be unusually important and certainly most confidential. Will you tell me now what it is?"[25]

Even though she resists confessing her motive, Maturin patiently leads her to reveal the whole story of her entanglement in a scheme that only her deep love for her husband, held hostage to her blackmailed compliance, could have brought into existence. He learns that the enemy's agents have identified *Surprise's* surgeon as one who has "corresponded in code" with certain interests in France, and that Laura is required "to win his confidence and obtain the addresses and the codes."[26] Stephen also persuades her to reveal the name of one of the contacts with whom she meets, although she refuses to describe his physical features, anxiously insisting that "she never would while Charles was in their hands: it might be unlucky. She would never do anything that might do Charles any harm."[27] Maturin attempts to dissuade her from looking upon himself, an ordinary naval physician, as one who would be capable of what the French agents have absurdly led her to believe, and he declares: "'I give you my sacred word of honour, I swear by the Four Gospels and my hope of salvation that you might have searched my papers for ever without finding a smell of a code or an address in France.' 'Oh,' she said, and he knew that although his words were literally true, she had pierced through to their essential falsity and that she did not believe *him*."[28] He reassures her by suggesting that he has an acquaintance "whose occupation brings him into touch with confidential affairs,"[29] and it is likely her would-be blackmailers have relied on informants who confused their identities. In this and in other ways Stephen quietens her fears, while also suggesting that his acquaintance could supply some of the information her tormenters want, since he is a man who, like Stephen, will be willing to aid a woman who is so lovingly dedicated to her husband's well-being.

In this manner O'Brian sets the stage for a plot in *Treason's Harbour* wherein Stephen contrives to satisfy the French agents that Mrs. Fielding has indeed been successful in seducing and compromising him, while he uses her as a conduit to feed them plausible but misleading intelligence. She accommodates to her role as an amateur double-agent with a mixture of anxiety and grit, driven by the fear that a blunder on her part could mean her husband's death. Once the charade is set in motion, Stephen manages his pupil's efforts with skill; nevertheless, *he* fears all the while that Lieutenant Fielding may already have been killed, despite the letters from her husband that Lesueur contrives to provide Laura in order to keep her hopes refreshed. Maturin also knows that before this deadly game is over, Fielding's courageous wife will have to be extricated from Malta with perfect timing, certainly prior to the moment Lesueur finds her no longer valuable and decides to end her life. Throughout the lengthy, high-stakes masquerade, she persists with an unflagging optimism and courage that steadily deepens Stephen's affectionate admiration for her.

Unknown to Maturin, Charles has in reality escaped from Bitche. He has been making a treacherous journey overland toward the sea and freedom, a trek that will take him well over two months to complete, and Fielding will be the only one of three escapees to survive the brutal ordeal. As the lieutenant nears the end of his odyssey, the *Surprise* weighs anchor to embark upon a brief mission across the Mediterranean with Maturin aboard. When his ship happens to encounter *H.M.S. Nymphe* off Trieste, he is informed that a fellow surgeon requires help in removing a bullet from the shoulder of a naval officer, one who has been rescued from a small rowboat and—in a most improbable circumstance—taken aboard his own former ship near Cape Promontore. Unfortunately, although this officer had initially been in high spirits after the rescue, "some busy fool acquainted with Valletta gossip" had told him that "his wife had not been quite discreet . . . and with whom."[30] The patient is, obviously enough, Charles Fielding, and the "whom" in the now deeply melancholy lieutenant's mind is Jack Aubrey.

After the surgery is successfully accomplished, Stephen listens as the patient describes his harrowing quest for freedom in detail. Lieutenant Fielding then concludes his narrative by grimly asking Dr. Maturin to deliver Captain Aubrey a handwritten message containing a barely disguised challenge to a duel. Acting as quickly as possible, Stephen delivers the letter and has no trouble persuading Jack to sail *Surprise,* without delay, back to Malta—where assassins will undoubtedly be eager to dispense with Laura as soon as the news of Charles Fielding's return reaches their ears. Immediately upon finding her again in Valletta, Maturin reveals both the good news of her husband's restoration to his ship and the darker news of Laura's own desperate position, hurriedly spiriting her out of the town and into safe haven aboard the *Surprise.* When he also tells her about Charles's determination to seek vengeance for being cuckolded by Jack Aubrey, her response is remarkably untroubled, and even cheerily confident: "[She] knew Charles very well; she had not the least doubt that she could deal with the situation as soon as they met; and at present all that she needed to make her perfectly happy was to see him again. No wonder she glowed so as to rival the lamp."[31] Because Laura has already proven her unflinching courage, Maturin shows no serious reluctance to put his faith in her understanding of Charles Fielding's psyche. Once the husband and wife are reunited, she is truly able to unburden her spouse's mind of suspicion and jealousy with ease.

Thus, as the novel's complex tale draws to a close, a blessedly positive outcome unfolds very quickly, and the ideal domestic harmony of the couple's marriage is firmly reestablished. Lieutenant Fielding and his faithful wife soon are expressing immeasurable gratitude to both Jack and Stephen for their vital aid, and the near-tragedy has resolved itself happily, however improbably, in the manner of a Shakespearean comedy of errors.[32] The story's various strands have been woven in such an intricate, slight-of-hand fashion that the plot of *Treason's Harbour* suggests a cat's cradle of puzzlement, one that is nevertheless capable of being dissipated in a graceful flick of Laura Fielding's wrists.[33] It is as if O'Brian is here mocking his own dedication to unflinching realism, and he appears to have taken delight in producing a victory for Laura that subjects Dr. Maturin's Age of Reason mentality to a challenging dose of a romance novelist's version of *kismet.*

Subtle self-mockery is in fact one of the characteristics that O'Brian's readers have often found endearing in his authorial posture. As Thomas Farrell has recently noted, O'Brian continually blends the mimetic with the diegetic,[34] persistently committing himself to veridical representation of a realistic, tangible world that is grounded in historical truth: a world inhabited by people who speak—and are immersed in—the distinctive, genuine English of the Napoleonic era, in a remarkable multiplicity of varieties. Yet he continually employs the shaping power of imagination to the figurative recounting of events and their interpretation, and this often involves ironical interplay between the mimetic reporting of dialogue (as well as interior monologue) and the diegetic blending of a character's interpretation of events with the author's selectively omniscient clarifications. Commenting on such an instance in another of O'Brian's novels, Farrell proposes, "While nothing disturbs the façade of mimetic accuracy, what we get [on such occasions] is actually an authorial joke at the 'truthiness' of his earlier fictions."[35] I believe this insight also applies to the concluding passages of Laura Fielding's story, where Stephen the consummate rationalist is carried to the proverbial "happy ending" in Laura's realm perhaps not so much by cool calculation, by *his* sophisticated application of critical and skeptical analysis, as it is by *her* simple, innocent invocation of the power of love.

CONCLUSION

In summary, then, six fictional characters created by Patrick O'Brian—Diana Villiers, Dil, the two Sweetings sisters, Clarissa Oakes, and Laura Fielding—provide ample evidence of the complexity and intersectionality of social, political, and cultural forces that impacted the lives of women and girls during the Napoleonic era. At the same time, the six are celebrations of the capacity for individual self-actualization in defiance of what might appear to be an irresistible destiny. Except in the tragic case of Dil, these unforgettable females persist and survive, even prosper, by means of psychological and emotional resilience, dogged resistance, and perhaps also by good luck. Yet, as "Lucky Jack" Aubrey fully realizes, this is "not chance, commonplace good fortune, far from it, but a different concept altogether, one of an almost religious nature, like the favour of some god or even in extreme cases like possession; and if it came in too hearty it might prove fatal—too fiery an embrace entirely. In any event it had to be treated with great respect, rarely named, referred to by allusion or alias, never explained."[36]

At times in an "almost religious" sense, O'Brian has framed his stories about significant women and girls as if they were part of a much larger theater of human life, which indeed they are. As Hugh Crago has observed, "Perhaps [any] story is a kind of analogical representation, in language, of the evolutionary process [of life] itself? The experience of story puts us in direct relationship with something purposeful yet mysterious, unpredictable yet patterned, new, yet old—a [microcosmic] encapsulation of mind within nature."[37] Aubrey's appreciation of the mystery at the heart of life's evolving drama supplies him with one of the vital credentials to become an agent of uncommon "good fortune," and to assist several female characters to become its beneficiaries. His intuitive wisdom is coupled with the gritty fortitude to persist in protracted struggles against daunting odds, and these characteristics link Aubrey and his "particular friend" in a saga of heroic dimensions. In O'Brian's twenty novels they share a commitment to redress wrongs done to the innocent and the powerless, and to do so without any narcissistic, hubristic certainty of victorious outcomes. Both Aubrey and Maturin exhibit an empathetic capacity to perform acts of generosity and selflessness elevating them well above the chauvinism and sexism of their day, endowing them with a kind of nobility that we still long to see in our own time. Their humane acts are often performed on behalf of women and girls who themselves demonstrate the heroic strength and courage of true warriors, wholly committed to their struggle against unjust fates. And all of them surely have reason to applaud the enlightened champion of scientific, humanistic rationalism befriending them, Dr. Stephen Maturin, as he strives throughout the O'Brian cycle to liberate bodies, minds, and spirits of men, women, and children from tyranny and suffering.

NOTES

1. Naval surgeons of the era were often little more than "sawbones," but Dr. Maturin's credentials compare favorably with the best medical practitioners of the early nineteenth century. Cf. J. Worth Estes, "Stephen Maturin and Naval Medicine During the Age of Sail," contained in Dean King's *A Sea of Words*, 3rd ed. (New York: Owl Books, 2000), 31–50.
2. Patrick O'Brian, *H.M.S. Surprise* (New York: W. W. Norton & Company, Inc., 1973), 194–95.
3. O'Brian, 217.
4. O'Brian, 237–38.
5. Diana of myth was not only goddess of the moon, but a huntress—wise, wily, and wild. She brought light into the world, protected virgins, and yet remained an untamable force. Maturin is drawn to his own Diana's irresistible brightness from *Post Captain* onwards; her immediate willingness to bond with the virginal Dil in *H.M.S. Surprise* gives him joy and hope; but, over the course of several more novels in the series, her essentially ungovernable nature defies his best efforts to link Diana's realm securely with his own. This kind of metaphorical layering is persistent throughout the Aubrey/Maturin *magnum opus*, a topic that has not yet been fully explored in O'Brian criticism.
6. Sophocles, *Oedipus Tyrannus*. Trans. By Peter Meineck and Paul Woodruff (Indianapolis: Hackett Publishing Company, Inc., 2000).
7. Patrick O'Brian, *The Nutmeg of Consolation* (New York: W. W. Norton & Company, Inc., 1992), 203–17 and *passim*.
8. O'Brian, 208.
9. Barret Bonden, Aubrey's coxswain, utters this phrase as the last words of the eighth novel, *The Ionian Mission*. The *Surprise* has just outfought a potent Turkish warship, *Torgud*, and after Jack's men board and force its surrender in bloody combat, hand to hand, he is warned: "'You had better get back to the barky, sir,' said Bonden in a low voice, tucking the ensign and the other officers' swords under his arm. 'This here is going to Kingdom Come.'" (New York: W. W. Norton & Company, Inc., 1994), 367.
10. This was a common epithet of the time, "file" being derived from Latin *filius* (or French *fils*), "son." Stephen is also conscious of his own self-contradictory position as an Irish Catholic serving under a flag whose officers are required to forswear "popery." Yet the greater evil, Napoleon, persuades him to accept the double standard for the greater good.
11. Charles Maturin, *Melmoth the Wanderer* (London: Penguin Books, Ltd., 2000).
12. J. Worth Estes, "Stephen Maturin and Naval Medicine During the Age of Sail," contained in Dean King's *A Sea of Words*, 3rd ed. (New York: Owl Books, 2000), 43.
13. Patrick O'Brian, *The Letter of Marque* (New York: W. W. Norton & Company, Inc., 1994), 271–77.
14. In King James translation: "Get thee behind me, Satan!" Patrick O'Brian, *The Commodore* (New York: W. W. Norton & Company, Inc., 1994), 107.
15. O'Brian, *The Nutmeg of Consolation*, 264. The harsh reality of life in the Australian penal colony is vividly detailed in James Tucker's *Ralph Rashleigh*. Tucker's contemporary descriptions fully validate the cheerless words of O'Brian's Jemmy Ducks.

16. O'Brian, 271.

17. Patrick O'Brian, *The Truelove* (New York: W. W. Norton & Company, Inc., 1992), 39.

18. This is a district in London where many "gentlemen's clubs" were located during the era of the Napoleonic wars. Clarissa states that Mother Abbott's was located "rather beyond the other side of the road," as she puts it. She also tells Stephen that she "always had a kindness for Black's"—Stephen's own club—"because it was a member that begged me off when I was to be hanged." O'Brian, 166.

19. O'Brian, *The Truelove*, 245.

20. This novel, by the way, was originally *Clarissa Oakes* when published in England, but was renamed for American audiences, perhaps because its former title would have echoed too much of Defoe, Richardson, or Austen. The *Truelove* is a British whaling ship first taken by a French privateer and subsequently retaken by the *Surprise*. Whimsical and romantic naming of ships was typical during the age of sail, so O'Brian could reiterate the linkage between liberation and powerful human affection here without surrendering himself to sentimentality.

21. Patrick O'Brian, *Post Captain* (New York: W. W. Norton & Company, Inc., 1994), 22. ("[Sophia] was a reserved creature, living much in an inward dream whose nature she did not communicate to anyone. Perhaps it was her mother's unprincipled rectitude that had given her this early disgust for adult life. . . ," which, in Mrs. Williams' home, always featured "an atmosphere of genteel money-worship, position-worship, and suffused indignation . . . .")

22. O'Brian, *Treason's Harbour* (New York: W. W. Norton & Co. 1994), 25–26.

23. O'Brian, 82.

24. O'Brian, 39.

25. O'Brian, 89.

26. O'Brian, 90.

27. O'Brian, 91.

28. O'Brian, 92. My italics.

29. O'Brian, 92.

30. O'Brian, 281. Mr. Thomas, Stephen's fellow physician, describes Charles Fielding's credulity-straining rescue in a garrulous way, concluding his embellished narrative as follows: "Rescued by his very own ship! If that ain't romantic, I don't know what romance is."

31. O'Brian, 309.

32. As O'Brian's reader has by now come to expect, the full account of this resolution is not to be accomplished until the first chapter of the ensuing novel, Patrick O'Brian, *The Far Side of the World* (New York: W. W. Norton & Co., 1994), 22–37.

33. O'Brian chose this quotation from Shakespeare's *Henry VI, Part Two*, Scene One, as the framing epigraph for the novel: "Smooth runs the water where the brook is deep; / And in his simple show he harbours treason." In O'Brian's novels, *simple* never means *shallow*.

34. Thomas J. Farrell, "The Diegetic Achievement of Patrick O'Brian," *Papers on Language and Literature*. Edwardsville. vol. 45, iss. 2 (Spring 2009), 150.

35. Farrell, "The Diegetic Achievement of Patrick O'Brian." 154. O'Brian would have applauded Farrell's use of Stephen Colbert's neologism, "truthiness." The mimetically meticulous novelist enjoyed taking occasional anachronistic liberties with vocabulary for wit's sake, as if he could not resist breaking free of historical exactitude for his own amusement—and for the opportunity to discover if any of his devoted readers would catch the jokester's "error."

36. Patrick O'Brian, *The Ionian Mission*, 268.

37. Hugh Crago, "'With a tale he cometh to you': A Phenomenological Journey to the Center of the Story," *Journal of the Fantastic in the Arts*. (International Association for the Fantastic in the Arts, 2018). vol. 29, no. 3. 440.

REFERENCES

Crago, Hugh. "'With a tale he cometh to you': A Phenomenological Journey to the Center of the Story." *Journal of the Fantastic in the Arts*. vol. 29, no. 3. International Association for the Fantastic in the Arts, 2018.

Estes, J. Worth. "Stephen Maturin and Naval Medicine During the Age of Sail," contained in Dean King's *A Sea of Words*, 3rd ed. New York: Owl Books, 2000. 31–50.

Farrell, Thomas J. "The Diegetic Achievement of Patrick O'Brian." *Papers on Language and Literature*. Edwardsville. vol. 45, iss. 2. Spring 2009. 150–79.

O'Brian, Patrick. *The Commodore*. New York: W. W. Norton & Co., 1994.

———. *The Far Side of the World*. New York: W. W. Norton & Co., 1994.

———. *H.M.S. Surprise*. New York: W. W. Norton & Company, Inc., 1993.

———. *The Ionian Mission*. New York: W. W. Norton & Company, Inc., 1994.

———. *The Letter of Marque*. New York: W. W. Norton & Company, Inc., 1988.

———. *The Nutmeg of Consolation*. New York: W. W. Norton & Company, Inc., 1992.

———. *Post Captain*. New York: W. W. Norton & Company, Inc., 1994.

———. *Treason's Harbour*. New York: W. W. Norton & Company, Inc., 1994.

———. *The Truelove*. New York: W. W. Norton & Company, Inc., 1992.

Maturin, Charles Robert. *Melmoth the Wanderer*. London: Penguin Books, Ltd., 2000.

Tucker, James. *Ralph Rashleigh*. Introduced and edited by Colin Roderick. London: The Folio Society, 1977.

Chapter Eight

A Distinct Set of Characteristics for Black Women at an HBCU

Tortured by Slavery-Shaped by Intersectionality-
Liberated into Othermothering

Sandra Williamson-Ashe

Multiple causes of oppression, race and gender, as well as other indicators of identity disadvantage black women. The notion of intersectionality supports that Black women have been both shaped and systemically suppressed. The shaped results of intersectionality among Black women began with slavery and now creates a benefit for HBCU (historically black colleges and universities) students. Black women provide university services for students that is delineated as going above and beyond the call of duty. Specific characteristics built from enslavement, shaped by intersectionality, uniquely coalesce to image othermothering.

Othermothering illustrates patterns of nurturing and cross-familial care that is prevalent in African American culture, and is also found in African American feminist literature.[1] The matrilineal care giving that creates othermothering is rooted in slavery and developed around the relationships of women and children.[2] Slavery emasculated the Black family structure by impeding marriage between Black men and women that colonial America depressed as property.[3] With the relentless looming fear of family separation, Black mothers adopted responsibility for motherless children[4] while being degendered and raped into breeders.[5]

The Black family is noted to be in ruins and deteriorating, but this view held by social theorist Moynihan, ignores the Black family's resilience and strength of kinship relations where the meaning of life and understanding of a common existence is learned.[6]

The dehumanizing violent institution of slavery mitigated the Black woman as invisible and mythicized her as promiscuous, animalistic, immoral, and inferior to white women; these beliefs continue to support stereotypical temperaments of modern day society.[7] Intersectionality is descriptive of the relationship between these identifiers and oppression.[8] An analysis of both physical and mental slavery, yields a Black woman's progression into areas of strength, esteemed as independence; self-identity; ideology and values; selflessness; preservation; and self-reliance. These characteristics may provide support for the matrilineal framework in othermothering.[9] proposes three fundamental components of othermothering, the ethic of care, cultural advancement, and institutional guardianship.

SLAVERY

The Negro family existed at the mercy of the slaveholder.[10] Families were allowed to survive as a profit-making necessity by the slaveholder; coupling to produce slave babies.[11] The slaveholder manufactured these families by joining mostly unrelated, non-blood relative slaves under one roof.[12] The slaveholder undercut all relational constructs to keep a sense of individual powerlessness and community oppression. Just as a pho-family was created by the slaveholder, the slave family used their familial edifice as strength to create individual and cultural strongholds.

As master, the slaveholder instigated intentional maltreatments on the slave family to remove the central operation from which oppositional activity originates, the slave woman.[13] At the commencement of the family, opposition begins with the slave woman reduced and stripped of femininity through the medieval practice of *jus primae noctis* ("the right of the first night"). In residence, slave women maintained the order of the household, provided meals, procreated children, and traditionally confirmed her inferiority through domestic labor.[14] This institutionalized abomination did not strangle, weaken, or enslave the internal strength of the physically slaved woman.

The Black woman was unshackled from the mythical feminist stance to aid the strategic promotion of slave labor and its ideologies.[15] From 1642–1864, the Black woman was the anti-slave rebel of the South.[16] Never sheltered or protected from the abuses, the slave woman was always the center of the survival-oriented resistance for slavery.[17] This survival is the pre-requisite for the callous noncompromising merciless struggles that created the Black woman's strengths, appreciated today as principals, navigators, artists, and architects.[18]

With no consideration for the resilience of the enslaved, the emancipation was considered a crisis because traditional ways of thinking were destroyed; slaves would have no restraint for their wild desires and impulses; and the crooked moral foundation established by the intimacy between slave and master was gone; this is known as Racial Scholarship.[19] As a result, twentieth century historians and social scientists examined Black and enslaved families through flawed models to justify their scientifically identified lower-class behavior.[20] One such sociologist was E. Franklin Frazier who noted that the plantation system was broken by the disruption of the slave order. Frazier domineeringly underestimated the capacities of slaves and ex-slaves, insisting the out-of-place slave order would render freed slaves with uninhabited impulses.[21] Without the master, there is no authority regulating sexual relations, and the relationship between mother and child or the sentiment between man and wife could not withstand the effects of freedom.[22]

Regardless of the slave experience, the commonality of experiences among Black women, passed-on from generations of household custodians, produced the ideologies for guidance and responsibilities in schools where they worked to advance the Black race in the midst of racial imbalance and oppression.[23] As their rich history and versatility would dictate, tirelessly African American Women (AAW) sought to ensure the gap between poor Black students and white supervisors was intentionally buffered.[24]

THE BLACK WOMAN

The experiences of Black women from slavery are reported by Davis (1971) to result in personality traits different from those of white women.[25] Today many Black women are void of knowing the depth of their lineage.[26] The deep lines of hard work and perseverance launches seekers of gender equity into a new womanhood.[27]

The stereotypes of Black women are venomous and practiced to justify oppressions that cultivate from labels of inferiority.[28] In the book, *Black Feminist Thought*, Collins (1990) identifies the stereotypes of Black women: Jezebel, Mammy, Matriarch, and Welfare Mother.[29] A jezebel lacks self-control for sexual impulses that lead white men into traps of wickedness.[30] A mammy takes care of everyone and ensures they follow and prioritize white supremacy.[31] A matriarch is despised by the children under her control and the men she emasculates.[32] The welfare mother (jezebel II) lacks morals or ethics in work and sex, and desires earning a living from a welfare check garnered through many and multiple sexual encounters that produce babies.[33] These racially-biased typecasts are not challenged by society but notably should be renounced by Black women.

As researchers of intersectionality note, uplifting all women is impossible when race is not amalgamated in understanding her experiences.[34] Applying the theoretical application of intersectionality to AAW, authorizes her validation and prevents her ostracism in the feminist movement.[35] The stereotypes

Collins (1990) identified for discussion are outside the lens of intersectional-ity and this penalizes a woman of color, unlike in the Kingdom of Dahomey where warrior women are valued, admired, and respected for their gifts.[36]

The strong Black women portrayed in the movie *Black Panther* mirror the real-life images of the true African all female military corps of Dahomey (now Benin), West Africa.[37] The French considered these African females, Amazonian warriors like those in Greek mythology.[38] Author Sylvia Serbin notes, there is no true category for these women who trained for a lifetime, were named according to their weapon expertise and unit assignment, sacri-ficed as the last line of defense for the king and bravely fought wars against French colonialism and the transatlantic slave trade.[39] Researcher John Hen-rik Clarke explained that prior to colonialism, the culture created by Africans was one in which the men were secure, and that security encouraged them to watch the flourishing woman grow uninhibited with her talents.[40] The notion of the female intellect being inferior is a European ideal from men, these men also perpetuated the superiority of the European women to the Black wom-an.[41] European labels intentionally highlight and build upon the oppression of the AAW.

The application of a strengths-based perspective unveils her gifts, talents, and abilities similar to the warrior women and better categorizes the AAW in an affirming position. The strengths-based approach concentrates on the in-herent strengths of a person. According to the principles of the approach, the primary focus in turn becomes the reality, including the language used, there-by an emphasis on strengths and not labels is the protocol.[42]

Incorporating social identity theory as explanatory framework, majority group members, considered the in-group, will discriminate against the out-group, the oppressed AAW.[43] This process is based on social categorization, the idea of them and us-social groups.[44] These ideals form a circular relation-ship with power and privilege. Black women, as "them," base their self-concept on how they are viewed by others, the mark of symbolic interaction-ism. Collins (1990) offers the need for an interlocking system comprised of race, class, and gender to fuel to the knowledge of assessing truth and elevat-ing subordinate groups about their own experiences that empower them to a new image of their reality.[45] Symbolic interactionism also positions that social roles are not fixed and can be interpreted in different ways.[46] Under-standing where Black women are in the power structure, labeling theory is clear that the ability of the powerful to impose their definitions on the power-less have tremendous consequences, even if the labels are not reality based.[47]

Using a strengths-based reflection; intentionally diminishes the impact of social identity theory; and removes symbolic interactionism as a lens for the Black woman's self-concept and replaces its use as fuel to remit the labelling theory, the oppressed Black woman will be redefined. With this application, the lens of African American women discussed by Collins (1990) can be extrapolated differently.[48] A jezebel could be relabeled an *Artist*. This too describes an AAW that thinks without limits, is exploratory, nonjudgmental, and optimistic, adapts to unanticipated surroundings, and she is creative with a broad focus. A mammy is as well positive in a different label, a *Principal*. This describes an AAW that assumes responsibility, she acts with vision based on high standards, and she creates a hospitable environment and a cooperative climate, and puts her needs aside enabling others to do their best. A Matriarch would be advanced as a *Navigator*. This AAW has vision to see ahead, is mentally engaged, attentive, and anticipates what was best for the success of others through their familial positions. Lastly, the most well-known of all, the welfare mother, is better radicalized as the *Architect*. This AAW mastermind, creates, is a problem-solver through design, considers safety in planning, and she appreciates new life and understands the growth necessary for change.

These traits can be had by any woman, but it is with clarity that the mold of slavery has established an outline and foundation for AAW to produce these confident characteristics, different from white women and this structural difference should be examined inclusive of the oppressive perils, but also with a discernment toward greatness.

INTERSECTIONALITY

The plight of intersectionality has been cultivated through three decades of civil rights and harmonious, anti-discrimination initiatives.[49] This movement advanced as women of color challenged being overlooked when feminist studies and theories were identified.[50] Black women were invisible; their complete existence went without acknowledgment.[51] The Black liberation movement responded to Blacks as Black men and Black women felt racially oppressed while the women's movement saluted women as white women leaving Black women to feel sexually oppressed.[52] Those groups with their own affiliations were unable to denounce Black women's oppression and invigorated the growth of the national Black feminist movement in the 1970s.[53] Black feminist scholar Kimberlé Crenshaw, a pioneer in the critical race theory, coined the term intersectionality and brought a resurgence to the Black feminist movement ideals; ideals also supported by sociologist Patricia Hills Collins, distinguished professor and author of many Black feminist literary works. Both Crenshaw and Collins honored the Black feminist movement in a crusade that refuses to permit oppression to conceal the intricacies and contributions of the AAW, intersectionality cannot be applied intermittently.[54] Mayberry (2018) remarks the same as many other researchers, there are a lack of studies isolating AAW of their race from other races and there is a lack of study regarding AAW in reference to their race and gender.[55]

Sanchez-Hucles and Davis (2010) indicate that intersectionality is partially defined by combining race and gender in differing manners to construct a social reality (as cited in Mayberry).[56]

THE AFRICAN AMERICAN WOMAN IN EDUCATION

The academy uses historical stereotypes to remedy Black women unpleasant and undesirable.[57] These stereotypes are translated into the social and scholarly marginalization that creates a barrier to prevent AAW from opportunities in higher education.[58]

First, scholarly marginalization standardizes certain scholarship lower and substandard within the institution, this research tends to focus on race-associated materials.[59] Secondly, the institution maintains a position with AAW by isolating her and insuring that she does not have the same professional development opportunities, thereby limiting her access to promotions.[60] Thirdly, selective incivility creates a barrier for AAW as they are revered as socially undervalued.[61] These actions reveal an intentional and universal unwritten policy to limit the influence AAW can have at the higher education table of decision-making and on the future directions of the college.

The institution proves itself to be academically obstructive and intentionally inhospitable toward the AAW. The biases against her stem from repeated stereotypes that have not diminished over time.[62] This is not surprising, the adoption of stereotypes act as a partition for which any related information is screened and selective recall begins regardless of the personal experiences lived that may have contradicted these beliefs.[63]

African American Women experience both racial and gender discrimination at the very institutions responsible for scholarly publications that rebuke the discriminatory practices that marginalize her as a Black woman.[64] The intellectual ideas of African American women are also being suppressed through the mainstream system of oppression, while the system of social control, an intentioned mass of polity, economy, and ideology is deliberately assigned to AAW to maintain their subordinance.[65]

Although the institution restricts AAW in leadership, there is a rich history of experiences and issues of race and gender where Black women create social change in the HBCU community and have an effect on advancement in the academy.[66] Black women make up 8 percent of the faculty population in higher education with HBCUs representing 3 percent of those institutions.[67]

HBCUs are known for creating an inclusive environment where faculty members develop noteworthy relationships with students.[68] Faculty member's interactions with students include support, engagement, development of university pride, and conduct and abilities for success.[69] And as noted, HBCU AAW faculty go above and beyond the call of duty, encouraging academic integration and persistence and social development and integration.[70]

At HBCUs, professionals see students as family and students see faculty as family; the importance of these relationships are valuable to the success of Black students in the HBCU community.[71] There is an expectation in the HBCU community that faculty go the extra mile. This expectation may be commanded as a result of the proven characteristics that accompany AAW. These characteristics are the result of ancestral lines of women made confident from Amazonian combats to the survival of slavery violations and the continuous evolution through labels of inferiority. The performance, above and beyond the norm, is the norm in the HBCU community and reveals the traditional roles of HBCU faculty that contain an identified value different from the traditional roles of non-HBCU faculty members.[72]

OTHERMOTHERING AND AN IDENTITY OF STRENGTH

The above and beyond, HBCU culture, resembles matrilineal nurturing and creates cross-familial patterns that equate to othermothering, a concept in African American feminist literature.[73] The concept is unique to AAW and is a direct descendant of slavery. The forced conditions of slavery, influenced family structures, and AAW readily cared for other's children for any length of time, hence the development of othermothering.[74] Othermothering is foundationally supported by three areas: the ethic of care, cultural advancement, and institutional guardianship.[75]

The inclusive climate created through faculty initiated personal relationships with students, foster a sense of belonging.[76] This nurturance is the ethic of care that shapes othermothering and encourages a support network for students.[77] Cultural advancement commits to advisement and mentorship that advances the lives of African American students.[78] Institutional guardianship represents the protection and preservation of the HBCU's cultural and intellectual capital; this knowledge is shared through the lines of mentorship between AAW faculty members and students.[79]

As othermothering connotes, AAW recognize the need to provide HBCU students with profound levels of understanding and attentive approaches.[80] In doing so, faculty members convey their personal investment in the students that look to them for mentorship.[81] With similar cultural experiences the result is a more self-assured student, confident in their ability to perform and behave according to the needs of their social environment.[82] Othermothering benefits HBCU student success though the proliferation of institutional satisfaction, commitment to goals, and academic achievement.[83]

African American Women executed othermothering by shadowing the culture of African traditions.[84] This cultural survival tool guaranteed that enslaved children would have their psychological and physical needs met through mothering.[85] Historically, othermothering was the primary vehicle for educating slave children and instilling them with a sense of cultural identification amidst the societal oppressions and victimizations.[86] The first construct of othermothering, the ethic of care, garners support through the HBCU familial relationships by forming close personal connections that improve academic and social integration for students, and this nourishes their ability to maximize their education and learning.[87] A sense of culture explored as cultural advancement, is the second construct of othermothering; it also develops through HBCU relationships. African American Women are encouraged to morally deliver values of sharing, caring, and accountability; in this Africentrism, AAW faculty share of themselves, provide an interactive-collective process, and deliver a spiritual association.[88]

"Othermothering in the academy . . . is guided by Africentric theory . . . principles of a holistic conception of people, a collective consciousness. . . ."[89] Increasingly, Black scholars are of the belief that the education of African American students requires "cultural reattachment," where every day African descendants adopt learned practices of African culture and focus education on the learning needs specific to African American students.[90] This is respective of Africentric theory because it centralizes Africans when analyzing African phenomena and the ideals and activities of African values and interests.[91]

Using the term *Africentrism* is an intentional reference to the continent of Africa from which African Americans are direct descendants.[92] This intentionality borders on linguistic appropriations seen prior to the extrapolation of strength-social-symbolism, discussed earlier in The Black Woman part 2 as an *Artist*, *Principal*, *Navigator*, and *Architect*. Linguistic appropriations permits the language of the oppressive group to be controlled by the dominant group.[93] Negative linguistics stereotype African Americans and the terms become instinctively linked with their social identity.[94]

Social identity theory, social categorization, symbolic interactionism, and labeling theory all posture the same powerless consequences of marginalized populations from dominant groups that have demoted the meanings of words to control language and linguistic appropriations. As a result of stereotypes and linguistic appropriations, AAW are categorized as jezebels, mammies, matriarchs, and welfare mothers. These stereotypical dialects of racism are psychological and social implants positioned to subdue the powerful characteristics of the AAW. These qualities are documented in research but the trajectory of the AAW must be intentioned and directed by the population most ostracized and oppressed with tones of intolerance, the African American Woman.

This intentional re-emphasis of the AAW's social disposition is powered through self-awareness and wisdom. The African American Woman recognizes her experiences and grasps the research indicating she educated and socialized the development of Black children for both their academic development and psychological growth; she assumed moral, ethical, and spiritual responsibilities for the children of others whether they were alone due to death, slave purchase, impoverishment, or ill prepared for motherhood; she advocated in segregated schools with a kinship that built parental collaborations and student advocacy; and she ordered firm student expectations through a holistic approach that empowered and advanced African American students with values and culture.[95]

It is categorically merciless and malevolent with full stratagem that society's majority group members have discriminated against the minority group members by reducing and omitting the true and victorious contributions of the AAW; this is social identity theory maneuvered. By not actively rejecting the labels of inferiority, there is support for the process of social categorization and compliance with social symbolism by centering their self-concept on the assessment of those in power and of privilege.

The subordinate descriptors of AAW—jezebels, mammies, matriarchs, and welfare mothers—should be socially re-categorized using the strengths perspective to mimic strength traits shaped from the perils of slavery. In contradistinction to the inferior terms, the AAW is characteristically defined as the *Artist, Principal, Navigator*, and *Architect*.

The attributing attributes of the *Artist, Principal, Navigator*, and *Architect,* are visible in the profile of othermothering. An *Artist* is oppressively referred to as a jezebel, the impulsivity and autonomy that characterizes them both promote conditions of othermothering. The impulsivity brings free flowing creativity that solves problems and autonomy encourages the sense of moral and social responsibility prevalent in othermothering. A *Principal* is depressively known as a mammy, high standards and empowerment are traits of both that are seen in othermothering. High standards and tough love with expectations are expressed through othermothering at HBCUs and students are empowered to excel. A *Navigator* is harshly mentioned as a matriarch, anticipation and relationships are visible in both as well as in othermothering. In anticipation, *Navigators* look to the present and future for preparation just as Othermothers and it is notable that relationships are critical to all aspects of othermothering. An *Architect* is unjustly referenced as a welfare mother, persistence and confidence are conditions present in both othermothering and the *Architect*. Confidently, HBCU AAW faculty members continuously attend to extending their sense of cultural connectedness to students. Griffin (2013) found that Black professors have a familial closeness, a sense of obligation and are committed to the development of Black students for their success.[96]

In a cyclic process, the inhumanities of slavery ignited the perils of racism that maintain current stereotypes. The stereotypes have aided in negative linguistic appropriations and masks the truly independent, self-assured, ideological, self-less, esteemed, and protective strengths of the AAW. The theoretical application of intersectionality to the societal lens of AAW filters away the toxins of false equality and encourages the precise identity of AAW, revealing their discounted strengths.

CONCLUSION

The scars of slavery, the complexities of intersectionality, influence the cultural and personal commitment of familial mentoring Black women develop and sustain with HBCU students. The othermothering that develops out of the underestimated AAW strengths that have evolved unrecognized is the norm of advisement at HBCUs. The AAW's strengths have been intentionally concealed beneath the colonial European stereotypes while her dignity has hoaxed as promiscuous, animalistic, and immoral, and her legacy mythicized as inferior to white women. Recognizing the immense contribution AAW have sustained in the collegiate success of HBCU students, it is imperative that the dehumanizing descriptors of her abilities are rejected and recreated to accentuate her true talents. The jezebel is justly an artist, the mammy is rightly a principal, the matriarch is correctly a navigator, and the welfare mother is truthfully an architect. This relabeling validates the AAW through a lens of intersectionality, removes the unethical ostracizing and punishments, and permissions her into her strength-based talents of othermothering.

NOTES

1. Joan Hirt, et al, "A System of Othermothering: Student Affairs Administrators' Perceptions of Relationships with Students at Historically Black Colleges." *National Association of Student Affairs Professionals* (2008): 210–23.
2. Hirt, 210–33.
3. Williams, Heather, "How Slavery Affected African American Families." Freedoms Story, TeacherServe. Accessed October 5, 2018. http://nationalhumanitiescenter.org/tserve/freedom/1609-1865/essays/aafamilies.htm.
4. Williams.
5. Hirt, "A System of Othermothering," 210–33.
6. Ruggles, Steven. "The Origins of an African-American Family Structure." *American Sociological Review* (1986): 136–51. http://users.hist.umn.edu/~ruggles/Articles/Af-Amfam.pdf; "The African American Family." Colonial Williamsburg: That the Future May Learn From the Past. http://www.history.org/almanack/life/family/black.cfm.
7. Ruggles.
8. Claire, "Intersectionality, Uncategorized." Sister Outrider. July 27, 2016. https://sisteroutrider.wordpress.com/2016/07/27/intersectionality-a-definition-history-and-guide/
9. Hirt, "A System of Othermothering," 210–33.

10. Angela Davis, "The Black Woman's Role in the Community of Salves." *The Black Scholar* (1971): 1–14. https://www.freedomarchives.org/Documents/Finder/DOC46_scans/46.RoleBlackWomenSlavery.pdf.
11. Davis.
12. Davis.
13. Davis.
14. Davis.
15. Davis.
16. Davis.
17. Davis.
18. Davis.
19. Herbert Gutman, *The Black Family in Slavery and Freedom, 1750–1925* (New York: Vintage Books 1976).
20. Gutman.
21. Gutman.
22. Gutman.
23. Sonya Horsford and Linda Tillman, *Intersectional Identities and Educational Leadership of Black Women in the USA*. New York: Routledge (2016).
24. Horsford and Tillman.
25. Davis, "The Black Woman's Role in the Community of Salves."
26. Sandra Miles, "Left Behind: The Status of Black Women in Higher Education Administration." (PhD diss., Florida State University Libraries 2012).
27. Miles.
28. Miles.
29. Patricia Collins, "Controlling Images and Black Women's Oppression." Nelsonssociology101, 1991. Accessed January, 2019, http://nelsonssociology101.weebly.com/uploads/2/6/1/6/26165328/controlling.pdf
30. Miles, "Left Behind."
31. Miles.
32. Miles.
33. Miles.
34. Claire, "Intersectionality, Uncategorized."
35. Claire.
36. Patricia Hill Collins, "Black Feminist Thought in the Matrix of Domination" in *Black Feminist Thought: Knowledge, Consciousness and the Politics of Empowerment* (Hartford Web Publishing 1990), 221–38, http://www.hartford-hwp.com/archives/45a/252.html.
37. Arica Coleman, "There's a True Story Behind Black Panther's Strong Women. Here's Why That Matters." *Time*, January 22, 2018, http://time.com/5171219/black-panther-women-true-history/.
38. Coleman.
39. Coleman.
40. Coleman.
41. Coleman.
42. Wayne Hammond, "Principles of Strength Based Practice" 2010, Alberta: Resiliency Initiatives, https://www.homelesshub.ca/resource/principles-strength-based-practice.
43. Saul McLeod, "Social Identity Theory." *Simply Psychology*, published 2008, https://www.simplypsychology.org/social-identity-theory.html.
44. McLeod.
45. Collins, "Black Feminist Thought in the Matrix of Domination."
46. Karl Thompson, "Social Action Theory-a Summary." *Revise Sociology*. July 13, 2016, https://revisesociology.com/2016/07/13/social-action-theory-a-summary/.
47. Thompson.
48. Collins, "Black Feminist Thought in the Matrix of Domination."
49. Janice Sanchez-Hucles and Donald Davis, "Women and Women of Color in Leadership: Complexity, Identity, and Intersectionality." *American Psychologist* 65, no. 3 (2010): 171–81.
50. Collins, "Black Feminist Thought in the Matrix of Domination."

51. "But Some of Us are Brave: A History of Black Feminism in the United States." Accessed January 15, 2019, https://www.mit.edu/~thistle/v9/9.01/6blackf.html.

52. Collins, "Black Feminist Thought in the Matrix of Domination."

53. Collins.

54. "Kimberlé Crenshaw on Intersectionality, More than Two Decades Later." Columbia Law School. June 8 2017, https://www.law.columbia.edu/pt-br/news/2017/06/kimberle-crenshaw-intersectionality.

55. Kena Mayberry, "African American Women Leaders, Intersectionality and Organizations" (PhD diss., Walden Dissertations and Doctoral Studies 2018).

56. Mayberry.

57. Miles, "Left Behind"; Mayberry, "African American Women Leaders, Intersectionality and Organizations."

58. Mayberry.

59. Mayberry.

60. Mayberry.

61. Mayberry.

62. AAUW, "Barriers and Bias, The Status of Women in Leadership," Published March 20 2016, https://www.aauw.org/research/barriers-and-bias/.

63. AAUW.

64. Mayberry, "African American Women Leaders, Intersectionality and Organizations."

65. Miles, "Left Behind."

66. Jean-Marie Gaetane and Virginia Cook Tickles, "Black Women at the Helm in HBCUs: Paradox of Gender and Leadership" in *In Black Colleges Across the Diaspora: Global Perspectives on Race and Stratification in Postsecondary Education* ed. Christopher Brown II and Elon Dancy II, (UK: Emerald Publishing Limited, 2018), 101–24.

67. AAUW, "Barriers and Bias, The Status of Women in Leadership."

68. Hirt et al., "System of Othermothering."

69. Hirt et al.

70. Hirt et al.

71. Hirt et al.

72. Hirt et al.

73. Hirt et al.

74. Hirt et al.

75. Hirt et al.

76. Hirt et al.

77. Hirt et al.

78. Hirt et al.

79. Hirt et al.

80. Hirt et al.

81. Alonzo Flowers III et al., "Beyond the Call of Duty: Building on Othermothering for Improving Outcomes at Historically Black Colleges and Universities" *Journal of African American Males in Education* 6, no. 1 (2015): 59–73.

82. Flowers III et al.

83. Flowers III et al.

84. Bernard, et al. 2012, "Othermothering in the Academy: Using Maternal Advocacy for Institutional Change" *Journal of the Motherhood Initiative for Research and Community Involvement* 3, no. 2 (2012): 103–20.

85. Bernard, et al.

86. Bernard, et al.

87. Hirt et al., "System of Othermothering."

88. Bernard, et al.

89. Bernard, et al.

90. Kmt Shockley, "Africentric Education Leadership: Theory and Practice" *International Journal of Education Policy and Leadership* 3, no. 3 (2008): 1–12.

91. Dwain Pellebon, "An Analysis of Afrocentricity as Theory for Social Work Practice." *Advances in Social Work* 8 no. 1 (2007): 169–83.

92. Augustine Nwoye, "An Africentric Theory of Human Personhood" *Psychology in Society* 54 (2017): 42–66.

93. Emily Hacala, "Language Appropriations," last modified March 6, 2011, http://languageasculturespring11.blogspot.com/2011/03/language-appropriation.html

94. Hacala.

95. Douglas Guiffrida, "Othermothering as a Framework for Understanding African American Students' Definitions of Student-Centered Faculty." *The Journal of Higher Education* 76, no. 6 (2005): 701–23.

96. Kimberly Griffin, "Voices of the "Othermothers": Reconsidering Black Professors' Relationships with Black Students as a Form of Social Exchange." *The Journal of Negro Education* 82, no. 2 (2013): 169–83.

REFERENCES

AAUW. "Barriers and Bias, The Status of Women in Leadership." *AAUW*. March 20, 2016. https://www.aauw.org/research/barriers-and-bias/.

"At the Intersection of Race and Gender Hatred." *Decolonizing Our History*. http://decolonizingourhistory.com/history-of-black-women-in-america-in-depth/.

Bernard, Wanda Thomas, Sasan Issari, Jemell Moriah, Marok Njiwaji, Princewill Obgan, and Althea Tolliver. "Othermothering in the Academy: Using Maternal Advocacy for Institutional Change." *Journal of the Motherhood Initiative for Reasearch and Community Involvement* 3, no. 2 (2012): 103–20.

"But Some of Us are Brave: A History of Black Feminism in the United States." *The Thistle*. Accessed January 15, 2019. https://www.mit.edu/~thistle/v9/9.01/6blackf.html.

Claire. "Intersectionality, Uncategorized." *Sister Outrider*. July 27, 2016. https://sisteroutrider.wordpress.com/2016/07/27/intersectionality-a-definition-history-and-guide/.

Coleman, Arica. "There's a True Story Behind Black Panther's Strong Women. Here's Why That Matters." *Time*. February 22, 2018. http://time.com/5171219/black-panther-women-true-history/.

Collins, Patricia Hill. 1990. *Black Feminist Thought, Knowledge, Consciousness, and the Power of Politics*. Abington, UK: Routledge, 1990. https://uniteyouthdublin.files.wordpress.com/2015/01/black-feminist-though-by-patricia-hill-collins.pdf.

Collins, Patricia Hill. "Black Feminist Thought in the Matrix of Domination." Hartford Web Publishing, 1990. http://www.hartford-hwp.com/archives/45a/252.html.

———. "Controlling Images and Black Women's Oppression." *Nelsonssociology101*, (1991). Accessed January 2019. https://nelsonssociology101.weebly.com/uploads/2/6/1/6/26165328/controlling.pdf.

Davis, A. "The Black Womans Role in the Community of Salves." *The Black Scholar* (1971), 1–14. https://www.freedomarchives.org/Documents/Finder/DOC46_scans/46.RoleBlackWomenSlavery.pdf.

Flowers III, Alonzo, Jameel Scott, Jamie. Riley, and Robert Palmer. "Beyond the Call of Duty: Building on Othermothering for Improving Outcomes at Historically Black Colleges and Universities." *Journal of African American Males in Education* 6, 1 (2015): 59–73.

Griffin, Kimberly. "Voices of the "Othermothers": Reconsidering Black Professors' Relationships with Black Students as a Form of Social Exchange." *The Journal of Negro Education* 82 (2013): 169–83.

Guiffrida, Douglas. "Othermothering as a Framework for Understanding African American Students' Definitions of Student-Centered Faculty." *Journal of Higher Education* 76, 6 (2005): 701–23.

Gutman, Herbert. *The Black Family in Slavery and Freedom, 1750–1925*. New York: Vintage Books, 1976.

Hacala, Emily. "Laguage Appropriation." *Language As Culture*, March 6, 2011. Accessed June 9, 2019. http://languageasculturespring11.blogspot.com/2011/03/language-appropriation.html.

Hammond, Wayne. *Principles of Strength Based Practice.* Alberta: Resiliency Initiatives, 2010. https://www.homelesshub.ca/resource/principles-strength-based-practice.

Hirt, Joan, Catherine Amelink, Belinda McFeeters, and Terrell Strayhorn. "A System of Other-mothering: Student Affairs Administrators' Perceptions of Relationships with Students at Historically Black Colleges." *National Association of Student Affairs Professionals* vol. 45, no. 2, (2008), 210–33.

Horsford, Sonya, and Linda Tillman. *Intersectional Identities and Educational Leadership of Black Women in the USA.* New York: Routledge, 2016.

Gaetane, Jean-Marie, and Virginia Cook Tickles. "Black Women at the Helm in HBCUs: Paradox of Gender and Leadership." In *Black Colleges Across the Diaspora: Global Perspectives on Race and Stratification in Postsecondary Education (Advances in Education in Diverse Communities: Research, Policy and Praxis)*, by C. Brown II and E. Dancy II, 101–24. UK: Emerald Publishing Limited, 2018.

"Kimberlé Crenshaw on Intersectionality, More than Two Decades Later." *Columbia Law School.* June 8, 2017. https://www.law.columbia.edu/pt-br/news/2017/06/kimberle-crenshaw-intersectionality.

Mayberry, Kena. "African American Women Leaders, Intersectionality and Organizations." Walden Dissertations and Doctoral Studies. December 22, 2018. https://scholarworks.waldenu.edu/dissertations/5221/.

McLeod, Saul. 2008. "Social Identity Theory." *Simply Psychology.* https://www.simplypsychology.org/social-identity-theory.html.

Miles, Sandra. "Left Behind: The Status of Black Women in Higher Education Administration." Florida State University Libraries, dissertation, 2012. Accessed January 23, 2019. http://diginole.lib.fsu.edu/islandora/object/fsu:183012/datastream/PDF/view.

Nwoye, Augustine. "An Africentric theory of Human Personhood." *Psychology in Society* 54, (2017): 42–66. http://www.scielo.org.za/pdf/pins/n54/04.pdf.

Pellebon, Dwain. "An Analysis of Afrocentricity as Theory for Social Work Practice." *Advances in Social Work* 8 (2007): 169–83. http://journals.iupui.edu/index.php/advancesinsocialwork/article/view/139.

Ruggles, Steven. "The Origins of an African-American Family Structure." *American Sociological Review* (1986): 136–51. http://users.hist.umn.edu/~ruggles/Articles/Af-Am-fam.pdf.

Sanchez-Hucles, Janice, and Donald Davis. "Women and Women of Color in Leadership: Complexity, Identity, and Intersectionality." *American Psychologist* 65, no. 3 (2010): 171–81. Accessed January 15, 2019.

Schockley, kmt. "Africentric Education Leadership: Theory and Pratice." *International Journal of Education Policy and Leadership* 3, no. 3 (2008): 1–12.

"The African American Family." Colonial Williamsburg: That the Future May Learn From the Past. http://www.history.org/almanack/life/family/black.cfm.

Thompson, Karl. "Social Action Theory-a Summary." *ReviseSociology.* July 13, 2016. https://revisesociology.com/2016/07/13/social-action-theory-a-summary/.

Williams, Heather. "How Slavery Affected African American Families." Freedoms Story, TeacherServe. Accessed October 5, 2018. http://nationalhumanitiescenter.org/tserve/freedom/1609-1865/essays/aafamilies.htm.

Chapter Nine

Forced Migration

Boko Haram's Induced Migration and the Plight of Women and Young Girls in Northern Nigeria

Mujtaba Ali Muhammad and Sa'ad Deen Sa'ad

Wars, terrorism, conflicts, and political instability are the major causes that lead to chaos, deaths, misery, squalor, famine, and forced migration worldwide; Boko Haram's insurgency led to the one of the worst humanitarian crises in Africa. Over 2.5 million people are displaced, while thousands were killed, maimed, and mutilated beyond recognition. Child soldiers were forcefully recruited into the militia, and in some cases women and girls were raped and abused in so many other ways. Many were killed, some by beatings, shootings, cuttings, some by stoning and some through forced suicide bombings by drugging them and strapping remotely detonated bombs on their bodies, others used as human shields. The term Boko Haram literally means "western education is forbidden,"[1] even though the sect rejects that name as derogatory. It was given to them by the media as stressed by Shekau, the sect leader preferring their self-selected name of Jama'atu Ahlussunna Lil Da'awati wal Jihad, meaning the people of the way of the prophet, for call to Islam and holy war. Another reason for the rise of insurgency is human rights abuse, mismanagement of lawlessness, excessive use of force, as evidenced by the way the group was first handled and subsequent extra judicial killing of their group leader, demolition of their houses and humiliation of others among them. This is the commonly believed version of events that many believed even then that it would lead to something horrible, which alas was the immediate cause of the start of the insurgency.[2]

HOW THE INSURGENCY FORCED
THESE VICTIMS INTO MIGRATION

Some victims experienced extreme terror leading to lack of viability of life in their usual environment, some lost their houses to arson by the members of Boko Haram, their male relatives murdered, the female folk raped. They were thoroughly harassed, intimidated, traumatized and in fear of recurring attacks. Boko Haram cut off their sources of livelihood by burning their farms and markets and making it unsafe for them to move about their normal lives, thereby inducing starvation. Schoolgoers were unable to go to school and the sick were unable to go to hospitals, because the schools and hospitals were operating on a minimal capacity and also because many were afraid to go out, and in some cases institutions were completely shut down. These conditions forced the inhabitants of these communities to abandon their houses seeking safer and more viable living environments. Sometimes they were even driven through direct violence to vacate their abodes without preparation, intention, or knowledge about where to go. Some saw gruesome sights of how their families, neighbors, and colleagues were massacred or violated. They migrated in fear of becoming victims, because the danger seems so imminent and they felt highly dejected it led them to give up and flee, as a consequence, they had sleepless nights and developed serious psychological conditions.

The Role Played by the Nigerian Army in
Forcing the Victims into Migration

According to Human Rights Watch, it "has previously documented 'wide-spread' abuses by the Nigerian security forces in response to Boko Haram attacks since 2009 security forces have used excessive force, burn homes, physically abused residents, 'disappeared' victims and extra judicially killed people suspected of supporting Boko Haram."[3] This led to the extent that the level of violence and abuse from the military was almost equivalent to that of Boko Haram; in fact, at one point the people feared the military more because they are ubiquitous and they hardly distinguish between friend and foe.

Socioeconomic Conditions of the IDPs in Camps and
Camp-Like Sites and Host Communities

The socioeconomic condition of these IDPs in their camps are dehumanizing; the camps lack basics such as water, clothing, electricity, toilet facilities, beds, mattresses, medications, and sufficient food. According to a survey conducted by NOI Polls shows "that the vast majority of IDP's in the North-East lack access to food, portable water, and healthcare." The survey further reveals that "almost 9 in 10 IDPs (85 percent) do not have access to quality food and regular meals, about 8 in 10 IDPs (78 percent) do not have access to potable water, while almost 7 in 10 IDPs (69 percent) lack access to quality healthcare."[4] It is also argued that the situation of these IDPs in the Northeast are similar in other camps nationwide. There was recently a report from the United Nations Children's Fund that "out of 244,000 children found to be suffering from acute malnutrition in Borno State, almost one in five, or roughly 49,000, would die if they failed to get quick medical assistance." The report also reveals that "Some 134 children on average will die every day from causes linked to acute malnutrition if the response is not scaled up quickly."[5] From the above description, one can see how deplorable these IDP camps are.

Psychological Trauma IDPs Went Through

One of the main outcomes of this forced migration is psychological trauma. Psychological is something less obvious than physical injury, which is quite debilitating. Also quite debilitating, however, was post-traumatic stress disorder (PTSD), depression, amnesia, which are all common outcomes for people who experienced psychological and sociological destruction of their homes, lives, and sudden loss of loved ones, and live in constant fear. These are all said to be risk factors for substance abuse, major depression, panic, discordant phobias, and PTSD.

In all these no one has suffered more than young girls although they are not the largest killed victim group of Boko Haram insurgents, even though they suffered physical abuse, forced labor, slavery, suicide bombing and rape, these things have physical and psychological consequences; they also suffered forced marriages, forced conversion, and other forms of psychological abuse. Human Rights Watch has documented some reports of how these IDPs suffered from traumatic psychological conditions;

> Many of the women and girls interviewed said that their experiences affected their psychological well-being. Some said they had difficulty sleeping, and deliberately isolated themselves to avoid insults and slurs. Many also said they felt constantly angry with their abusers, wishing they could harm them in retaliation. None said they had professional counselling.[6]

A 30-year-old woman from Gwoza said:

> I feel sad all the time. I am always thinking about all the bad things that have happened to me. Sometimes I cry; at other times I try to resign to my fate. But it is hard. My neighbors in the camp encourage me to pray. That is all I can do, pray.[7]

A 16-year-old rape survivor said she was always thinking about death, and wished she had the courage to kill herself.[8]

> Nobody comes to this camp to talk to us. We IDPs only have one another, but even that is hard because you do not know who to trust. If you tell them your secret pain or shame, they can use it to mock you later.[9]

Attacks, Theft, and Rape on IDP Camps Being Perpetrated by Boko Haram and Security Operatives

There have been several cases of attacks, theft, and rape documented by human right organizations, media, and police reports and from the word of mouth by the victims, statements of healthcare professionals, relatives of the victims, and other anecdotal evidences. For example, on February 9, 2015, there was an attack on Dikwa IDP camp by two female suicide bombers, which killed 58 IDPs, and an earlier attempt by another set of Boko Haram female suicide bombers at Dalori near Maiduguri which was thwarted by the security operatives. On January 17, 2017, another tragedy occurred in an IDP camp at Kala-Balge, a local government of Borno state, when military jets mistakenly bombed what they perceived as Boko Haram's hideout. A total of 234 people were killed as explained by the council's chairman. "We buried 234 corpses in Rann after the bombs were dropped on the IDP camp," Mr. Malarima said. "We have two others injured persons that died while in hospital in Maiduguri."[10]

Additionally, "In late July, 2016, Human Rights Watch documented sexual abuse, including rape and exploitation, of 43 women and girls living in seven internally displaced persons (IDP) camps in Maiduguri, the Borno State capital. The victims had been displaced from several Borno towns and villages, including Abadam, Bama, Baga, Damasak, Dikwa, Gamboru Ngala, Gwoza, Kukawa, and Walassa."[11]

Some of the most unfortunate rape cases were carried out by the security operatives who were supposed to protect these weak and vulnerable people. An example of abuse by police officers against an IDP as reported by HRW is as follows,

> A 17-year-old girl said that just over a year after she fled the frequent Boko Haram attacks in Dikwa, a town 56 miles west of Maiduguri, a policeman approached her for "friendship" in the camp, and then he raped her.[12]

Another example of rape by vigilante operative against a female IDP is as follows:

> A 16-year-old girl who fled a brutal Boko Haram attack on Baga, near the shores of Lake Chad, northern Borno in January 2015, said she was drugged

and raped in May 2015 by a vigilante group member in charge of distributing aid in the camp.[13]

An example of sexual exploitation by the Nigerian soldiers also demonstrates abuse by those who were sworn to protect their charges:

A 30-year-old woman from Walassa, near Bama, about 43 miles west of Maiduguri was "rescued" by the Nigerian government soldiers, and a Hausa soldier from Gwoza took advantage of her by promising to marry her and continue to have sex with her until when she got pregnant, he disappeared.[14]

According to Human Rights Watch, "Women and girls abused by members of the security forces and vigilante groups told Human Rights Watch they feel powerless and fear retaliation if they report the abuse." The fear of been killed, brutalized, labeled, or stigmatized usually prevent them from reporting their cases.[15]

THE FATE OF IDPS—ESPECIALLY THE YOUNG GIRLS

One of the most popular stories of Boko Haram's abductions was that of schoolgirls from Chibok and that of Dapchi towns. Shortly before writing their final exams on April 2014, about 276 Chibok schoolgirls were forcefully abducted from their school by the well-armed terror group Boko Haram, which was the beginning of their anguish; many of the schoolgirls are still with them.[16] Four years later, on February 19, 2018, another 110 school girls were kidnapped by Boko Haram members from Dapchi town, they were later released after negotiating with the government.[17]

These young girls were subsequently forced to convert, marry, and sold as slaves as claimed by Shekau, the leader of the dreadful group. Their condition has disrupted many aspects of their development, especially their education and their social relationships. It has cut them out from their social circles, peers and family, it has affected their self-esteem, shattered their dreams and has reduced the chances of unmarried among them from having a spouse of their choice and separated those that are from their spouses. Because of the disruption of their education, it has created a gap in their earning potential from what they can become and what they are now, as well as in relation to their peers who are unaffected by the insurgency. Their integration into society is going to be a serious challenge because of the mixed opportunity and the excess baggage they come with. Their future appears bleak even when they get out of the IDP camps, unless a multi-faceted and concerted effort is made to thoroughly integrate them back into society; the future of the abducted among them is even much less certain.

CONCLUSION

To alleviate the conditions of the migrants a number of measures have to be taken by all the stakeholders, namely, governments at all levels, international, national, and other humanitarian agencies, host communities, NGOs, CBOs, faith-based organizations, philanthropists, and individuals. Firstly, there is a need for the Nigerian government to provide adequate protection for the IDP camps from attacks by Boko Haram insurgents. The government must make provisions for basic amenities, such as good health care services, enough nutritious food, and hygienic water supply for the migrants to live a fairly decent life in the IDP camps. Security operatives and camp personnel who are found guilty of various offenses including rape, abuse of children, theft, etc., must be punished to serve as a deterrence to others. An up-to-date and sustainable enumeration of migrants must be put in place; this will help in keeping statistics. Additionally, routine training for the camp officials and other people involved in camp maintenance should be established. Nigeria, as a signatory of Kampala AU-Convention on Internally Displaced Persons, must implement in full all the provision therein including article nine, which states the obligations of the signatory states in relation to protection and assistance to Internal Displacement, which states that:

> States Parties shall protect the rights of internally displaced persons regardless of the cause of displacement by refraining from, and preventing, the following acts, amongst others:
>
> a. Discrimination,
> b. Genocide,
> c. Arbitrary killing, summary execution, arbitrary detention, abduction,
> d. Sexual and gender based violence in all its forms, notably rape,
> e. Starvation.[18]

Deep-seated solutions need to be implemented at the macro level. This should include socioeconomic empowerment of the highly deprived classes of the deprived zones which constitute the most fertile recruitment grounds of the insurgency. This should come in the form of education, skill acquisition, and economic opportunities to the widest possible numbers covering the whole zone. It should be done along with a social reorientation component and a comprehensive and humanizing Islamic religious reeducation that will teach them to be tolerant, community oriented, positive, humane, and civilized members of society.

NOTES

1. Human Rights Watch, "Spiraling Violence: Boko Haram Attacks and Security Abuses in Nigeria" (accessed March 6, 2017) https://www.hrw.org/report/2012/10/11/spiraling-violence/boko-haram-attacks-and-security-force-abuses-nigeria.

2. Human Rights Watch.

3. Kampala Convention African Union Convention for the Protection and Assistance of Internally Displaced Persons in Africa. https://au.int/sites/default/files/treaties/36846-treaty-0039_-_kampala_convention_african_union_convention_for_the_protection_and_assistance_of_internally_displaced_persons_in_africa_e.pdf.

4. Human Rights Watch, "Nigeria: Officials Abusing Displaced Women and Girls" (accessed January 10, 2017) https://www.hrw.org/news/2016/10/31/nigeria-officials-abusing-displaced-women-girls. NOIPolls, "Most IDPs Suffer From Lack of Food, Potable Water, and Healthcare" (accessed February 1, 2017) https://noi-polls.com/most-idps-suffer-from-lack-of-food-potable-water-and-healthcare/.

5. Human Rights Watch; NOIPOLLS, "Most IDPs Suffer From Lack of Food, Potable Water, and Healthcare."

6. Human Rights Watch.

7. Human Rights Watch.

8. Human Rights Watch.

9. Human Rights Watch.

10. Human Rights Watch.

11. Human Rights Watch.

12. Human Rights Watch.

13. Human Rights Watch.

14. Human Rights Watch.

15. Human Rights Watch.

16. "Boko Haram Kidnapped 276 Girls Two Years Ago: What Happened To Them?" *Washington Post* (accessed May 7, 2016) https://www.washingtonpost.com/news/worldviews/wp/2016/04/14/boko-haram-kidnapped-276-girls-two-years-ago-what-happened-to-them/.

17. British Broadcasting Corporation, "Nigeria Dapchi Abductions; Schoolgirls Finally Home" (accessed May 2, 2018) https://www.bbc.com/news/world-africa-43535872.

18. Human Rights Watch, "Spiraling Violence."

REFERENCES

African Union. "African Union for the Protection and Assistance of Internally Displaced Persons in Africa" (accessed April 5, 2015) https://au.int/sites/default/files/treaties/36846-treaty-0039.

British Broadcasting Corporation. "Nigeria Dapchi Abductions; Schoolgirls Finally Home" (accessed May 2, 2018) https://www.bbc.com/news/world-africa-43535872.

"Boko Haram Kidnapped 276 Girls Two Years Ago: What Happened To Them?" *Washington Post* (accessed May 7, 2016) https://www.washingtonpost.com/news/worldviews/wp/2016/04/14/boko-haram-kidnapped-276-girls-two-years-ago-what-happened-to-them/.

Human Rights Watch. "Spiraling Violence: Boko Haram Attacks and Security Abuses in Nigeria" (accessed March 6, 2017) https://www.hrw.org/report/2012/10/11/spiraling-violence/boko-haram-attacks-and-security-force-abuses-nigeria.

Human Rights Watch "Nigeria: Officials Abusing Displaced Women and Girls" (accessed January 10, 2017) https://www.hrw.org/news/2016/10/31/nigeria-officials-abusing-displaced-women-girls3.

Kampala Convention African Union Convention for the Protection and Assistance of Internally Displaced Persons in Africa, https://au.int/sites/default/files/treaties/36846-treaty-0039_-_kampa-

la_convention_african_union_convention_for_the_protection_and_assistance_of_internally
_displaced_persons_in_africa_e.pdf.

NOIPOLLS. "Most IDPS Suffer From Lack of Food, Potable Water, and Healthcare" (accessed
February 1, 2017) https://noi-polls.com/most-idps-suffer-from-lack-of-food-potable-water-
and-healthcare/.

Index

About the Editors

Dawn L. Hutchinson has taught for the philosophy and religion department at Christopher Newport University in Newport News, Virginia, since 2004. She specializes in American religious history, with particular emphasis on new religious movements. Her most recent book is entitled *Secret of Success: The Link between American Prosperity Theology and Business Self-Help Literature* for NOVA Science Publishers. Areas of academic interest include new religious movements, feminism, African American religious history, gender/religion, gnosticism, new thought, transcendentalism, and the social gospel.

Lori J. Underwood is professor of philosophy and dean of the College of Arts & Humanities at Christopher Newport University. Her areas of research include Kant studies, social, and political philosophy, gender studies, philosophy of law, and terrorism studies. She is the author of numerous books and articles and her most recent scholarship focuses on cosmopolitanism, intersectional identity, and terrorism.

About the Contributors

Jason Ray Carney is a lecturer in the Department of English of Christopher Newport University in Newport News, Virginia. He is the co-editor of the academic journal *The Dark Man: Journal of Robert E. Howard and Pulp Studies* and the area chair of the "Pulp Studies" section of the Popular Culture Association. He is the author of *Weird Tales of Modernity: The Ephemerality of Ordinary in the Stories of Robert E. Howard, Clark Ashton Smith, and H. P. Lovecraft* (McFarland 2019).

James Cornette has been a member of the CNU English Department's regular faculty for over thirty years, during which time he has taught a wide variety of classes in the literature and language arts curricula, including the history and structure of the English language. His undergraduate and graduate studies focused on eighteenth- and early nineteenth-century English and American literature, history, and philosophy, and the combination of these academic interests has made the Aubrey/Maturin novels of Patrick O'Brian (1914-2000) an enduring fascination for him. His ability to capture the authentic voices of the era of the Napoleonic Wars throughout the course of twenty novels, and to do so with the sophisticated skills of a master prose stylist and penetrating analyst of human nature, has earned O'Brian preeminent stature among writers of historical fiction.

Patricia Hopkins received her PhD and MA from the University of Pennsylvania in Philadelphia, and her BA from Queens College, CUNY, in Flushing, NY; is the director of African-American studies as well as an associate professor in the English Department, with a specialization in African American studies at Christopher Newport University. In addition to deconstructing images of African Americans and Black life in the media, Dr. Hopkins' research interests include African American literature and gender studies, specifically looking at the violence inflicted upon the Black female body in the cases of sexual exploitation, rape, and lynching. More specifically, her work shows that the rape of white women and lynching of black men tell only a part of the story, when one looks at the horrors inflicted upon the human body in literature. She examines the importance of breaking the institutional silence by adding the plight of black women to the discourse of narrative violence.

Gaius Jatau is an associate professor of economic and political history. He is a senior lecturer in the Department of History, Kaduna State University, Kaduna, Nigeria. Jatau has served and still serving the university in different committees and associations. His primary responsibilities include teaching and research. He supervised both undergraduate and postgraduate projects and theses. He has published numerous articles in local and international journals, chapters in books, and authored a published book titled *The Colonial Economy of Jema'a, 1900–1960.*

Mujtaba Ali Muhammad studied at the College of Arts and Science Kano and Ahamadu Bello University Zaria. Muhammad did postgraduate work at Bayero University Kano and is enrolled in the PhD Program in public policy and administration at Walden University. Muhammad recently founded an NGO named IDPS HOME which focuses on women, young girls, and childrens' welfare, human rights, shelter, education, and security.

Geovani Ramírez is a PhD candidate in the Department of English and Comparative Literature at the University of North Carolina at Chapel Hill, where he specializes in multiethnic and latinx US literatures. His dissertation explores the ways Mexican-heritage women writers use the topic of labor in their works to interrogate and re-shape notions of class, race, gender, culture, (trans)national identities, and citizenship. Geovani is a graduate assistant for the UNC latina/o studies program. While at UNC, Geovani has enjoyed working with UNC students in various capacities, including as sole instructor for both composition and literature courses. He has been a graduate research consultant for classes in the UNC department of women's and gender studies and the latina/o studies program, a graduate fellow at the UNC Center for Faculty Excellence, and an assistant writing coordinator for the Moore Undergraduate Research Apprentice Program. Geovani has also worked as a writing coach at the UNC Writing Center, where he helped undergraduate and graduate students from all disciplines working on a wide range of writing genres and projects.

Sa'ad Deen Sa'ad was born in 1973 in Kano State. He attended Science Secondary School Dawakin Kudu Kano, and also attended ABU Zaria and BUK Kano. He writes academic papers on various disciplines including medicine, education, philosophy, religious studies, business administration, etc. He is currently a research fellow with Aminu Kano Specialist Hospital, Kano.

Ursula Scheidegger is a researcher at the University of the Witwatersrand, Johannesburg, South Africa. Her PhD is in political studies from the University of the Witwatersrand in Johannesburg, South Africa. She is a researcher in different projects; her areas of interests are women's rights, prevention of violence against women, gender equality, democracy, participation and representation, local government, public space and urban development. She is consultant to different non-governmental organizations.

Sandra Williamson-Ashe has been an assistant professor at Norfolk State University in the Ethelyn R. Strong School of Social Work for 5 years, where she also received her MSW; her BS is in criminal justice from UNC-Charlotte. With a doctorate in higher education administration and leadership from the George Washington University, she has served in several senior level university administrative positions; assistant to the director of the higher education center and distance education, associate vice president for student affairs, and vice president for enrollment management and student affairs. Previously she served as a gubernatorial appointment to the Council on Aging and a Virginia Beach mayoral appointment to the e-gov commission. Her research interests include student persistence, integrity, social work pedagogy, leadership, and the leadership of women in higher education.

www.ingramcontent.com/pod-product-compliance
Lightning Source LLC
Chambersburg PA
CBHW022323280326
41932CB00010B/1204